Longman School
Shakespeare

D1395718

The Merchant of Venice

Editor: John O'Connor
Textual Consultant: Dr Stewart Eames

Volume Editor: John O'Connor

GCSE Assessment Practice:
Margaret Graham (WJEC)
Chris Sutcliffe (AQA)
Pam Taylor (Edexcel)
John Reynolds (OCR)

Longman
Part of Pearson

Longman is an imprint of Pearson Education Limited, a company incorporated in England and Wales, having its registered office at
Edinburgh Gate, Harlow, Essex, CM20 2JE.
Registered company number: 872828

www.pearsonschoolsandfecolleges.co.uk

Longman is a registered trademark of Pearson Education Limited

First published 2010

12 11 10
10 9 8 7 6 5 4 3 2 1

British Library Cataloguing in Publication Data
A catalogue record for this book is available from the British Library.

ISBN 9781408236901

Typeset by Juice Creative Ltd, Hertfordshire
Cover photo © Photostage, Ltd.
Printed and bound in Great Britain by Henry Ling Limited, at the Dorset Press, Dorchester, DT1 1HD

We are grateful to the following for permission to reproduce copyright photographs:

Getty Image: *page 197*: Andrea Pistolesi/The Image Bank

Every effort has been made to contact copyright holders of material reproduced in this book. Any omissions will be rectified in subsequent printings if notice is given to the publishers.

CONTENTS

ACT 1: SCENE BY SCENE

1 Bassanio tells Antonio of his plans to woo Portia, and asks him for a loan to finance his trip to see her. Antonio is willing to lend Bassanio the sum he needs but, as Antonio's money is tied up in business ventures, he tells Bassanio to borrow it in his name.

2 Portia and Nerissa discuss the suitors who have come from all over the world in the hope of marrying Portia. They mention the method (a choice between three caskets) by which Portia must be won.

3 Bassanio asks Shylock for a loan of three thousand ducats. When Antonio arrives, he and Shylock argue about money-lending and interest. Shylock reminds Antonio how badly he has treated him in the past, but offers to lend the sum as an act of friendship and charge no interest. Instead, they agree that if Antonio is unable to pay back the loan on the agreed date, Shylock may take a pound of his flesh.

Act 2: scene by scene

1 The Prince of Morocco arrives at Belmont. Portia reminds him that he must choose the right casket.

2 After considering whether it is the right thing to do, Lancelot Gobbo decides to leave Shylock's service and informs his father. Bassanio takes Lancelot on as a servant, and then agrees to allow Gratiano to accompany him to Belmont.

3 Shylock's daughter, Jessica, says farewell to Lancelot and plans to run away from her father and to marry Lorenzo.

4 Lorenzo and his friends discuss how they will steal Jessica away during a masque that evening. Lancelot brings Lorenzo a letter from Jessica in which she tells him how she will disguise herself and take some of Shylock's gold and jewels.

5 Shylock is reluctant to leave his house to dine with Antonio and Bassanio. Finally he goes and Jessica prepares to run away.

6 Jessica steals some of Shylock's money and jewels and, having disguised herself as a boy, runs off with Lorenzo. Antonio arrives to tell Gratiano that Bassanio's ship is ready to set sail for Belmont.

7 The Prince of Morocco deliberates over the caskets and chooses gold. Finding that he has chosen the wrong casket, he quickly departs.

8 Salerio and Solanio describe Shylock's reaction to the discovery that his daughter has run away and stolen his jewels. They fear for Antonio if he is unable to repay the money he owes Shylock.

9 The Prince of Aragon, another suitor, picks the silver casket. Finding that he has chosen incorrectly, he too takes his leave. News comes of another suitor and Nerissa hopes that it might be Bassanio.

ACT 3: SCENE BY SCENE

1 Salerio and Solanio express great concern for Antonio, hearing that one of his ships has been lost. They taunt Shylock, who demands the pound of flesh owed him. Tubal arrives to report that, although he has been unable to find Jessica, he has heard that she has spent a great deal of Shylock's money.

2 At Belmont, Bassanio chooses the correct casket and Portia gives him a ring as a token of her love. Gratiano reveals that he and Nerissa also plan to marry. Salerio then arrives with Lorenzo and Jessica to report that Antonio is bankrupt and Shylock is demanding the pound of flesh. Portia tells Bassanio to go to help his friend.

3 Antonio pleads with Shylock to have mercy, but Shylock refuses to listen.

4 Portia appoints Lorenzo as master of Belmont in her absence and begins to reveal her plans to Nerissa. She sends her servant, Balthazar, to Padua to collect certain papers and clothes from her cousin, Doctor Bellario, and tells Nerissa that they will disguise themselves as young men.

5 Lancelot talks to make to Jessica about her having become a Christian. Lorenzo and Jessica discuss Portia's virtues.

Act 4: scene by scene

1 Appearing before the Duke's court, Shylock refuses appeals to him to show mercy and pursues his demand for a pound of Antonio's flesh. Portia arrives, disguised as a young lawyer, to try the case. She explains the nature of mercy to Shylock and, when he remains determined not to show any, uses Venetian law to prevent him from killing Antonio. Shylock is defeated and leaves the court forced to become a Christian and to make a will leaving everything to Lorenzo and Jessica. When Bassanio asks the young lawyer to accept a reward, Portia asks for the ring she gave him. At first he refuses, but he is then persuaded by Antonio, and sends the ring after her.

2 Outside the court, Gratiano catches up with Portia and gives her Bassanio's ring. Nerissa says she will also try to persuade Gratiano to give up the ring she gave him.

Act 5: scene by scene

1 At Belmont, Jessica and Lorenzo are sitting in the moonlight talking about lovers and music. Portia and Nerissa return, and Portia commands that no one should reveal that they have been absent. She welcomes Bassanio when he arrives with Antonio, but an argument quickly begins between Nerissa and Gratiano about the loss of his ring. Gratiano reveals that Bassanio has also given his ring away, and Portia forcefully reminds him of its true value. Returning the rings to their husbands, the women pretend that the young men to whom their husbands gave their rings have slept with them. Finally Portia reveals that she and Nerissa were the lawyer and clerk, and she gives Antonio a letter telling him that three of his ships have come safely home with rich cargoes. Lorenzo is also given the deed by which he learns that he and Jessica will inherit Shylock's wealth.

IN VENICE

ANTONIO
A merchant
He signs a bond with
Shylock to borrow
money for Bassanio.

BASSANIO
*A young lord and
friend of Antonio*
He chooses the right
casket and wins Portia.

SOLANIO
A friend of Antonio
With Solanio, he
taunts Shylock after
the loss of Jessica.

SALERIO
A friend of Antonio
He helps Lorenzo to
elope with Jessica and
brings news of Antonio's
plight to Belmont.

LEONARDO
Bassanio's servant
He is given
instructions
concerning Bassanio's
visit to Belmont.

LORENZO
A friend of Antonio
He elopes with Jessica
and takes charge of
Portia's house while she
is in Venice.

GRATIANO
A friend of Antonio
He accompanies
Bassanio to Belmont
and marries Nerissa.

SHYLOCK
*A wealthy Jew
of Venice*
He lends Antonio
money and demands
the pound of flesh
owed to him when
Antonio cannot repay
the loan.

TUBAL
Shylock's friend
Although unable to
locate Jessica, he
tells Shylock how
much she has been
spending and reports
Antonio's losses.

JESSICA
Shylock's daughter
She is in love with
Lorenzo and runs
away from her
father's house, taking
money and jewels
with her.

LANCELOT GOBBO
Shylock's servant
He leaves Shylock's
service to become a
servant of Bassanio.

OLD GOBBO
*Lancelot's more than
half-blind father*
He is teased by his son,
but then speaks up for
Lancelot when he applies
to Bassanio to become
one of his servants.

THE DUKE
He presides over the
trial in which Shylock
claims a pound of
Antonio's flesh.

At Belmont

Portia
A wealthy heiress
She is overjoyed when Bassanio chooses the correct casket. Hearing of Antonio's plight, she travels to Venice, disguises herself as a lawyer and defeats Shylock in court.

Nerissa
Portia's companion / lady-in-waiting
She marries Bassanio's friend, Gratiano, and accompanies Portia to Venice disguised as a lawyer's clerk.

Balthazar
Portia's servant
Portia sends him to her lawyer cousin, Doctor Bellario, in Padua, to fetch documents and clothing.

Stephano
Portia's servant
He tells Lorenzo and Jessica that Portia will shortly be returning to Belmont.

The Prince of Morocco
One of Portia's suitors
He chooses the gold casket, attracted by its richness.

The Prince of Aragon
One of Portia's suitors
Believing himself superior to the people who would choose gold, he selects the silver casket.

A Messenger
He tells Portia of the approach of a new suitor who turns out to be Bassanio.

IN VENICE

ANTONIO *a merchant*

BASSANIO *his friend*

SALERIO

SOLANIO

GRATIANO } *other friends of Antonio*

LORENZO

SHYLOCK *a wealthy Jew of Venice*

JESSICA *Shylock's daughter*

TUBAL *a friend of Shylock*

LANCELOT GOBBO *first Shylock's servant, then Bassanio's*

OLD GOBBO *Lancelot's father*

LEONARDO *Bassanio's servant*

DUKE OF VENICE

Antonio's Servant, Bassanio's other servants, a Jailer, Venetian Citizens, Lawyers and Court Officials

AT BELMONT

PORTIA *a rich heiress, lady of Belmont*

NERISSA *her waiting-woman/companion*

BALTHAZAR

STEPHANO } *her servants*

THE PRINCE OF MOROCCO

THE PRINCE OF ARAGON } *suitors to Portia*

A MESSENGER

Other servants, attendants and followers, Portia's singers and musicians

The scenes are set in Venice, and at Portia's house of Belmont.

In this scene ...

- Bassanio tells Antonio about the rich heiress, Portia.
- Antonio promises to lend Bassanio the money he needs to woo Portia.
  His money is tied up but he tells Bassanio to borrow money in his name.

Antonio's friends, Salerio and Solanio, ask him why he is sad. They suggest that he might be worried about the safety of his ships and the rich cargoes they carry.

THINK ABOUT for GCSE

Performance and staging

- In his opening line, Antonio declares that he is 'sad'. In what ways might an actor's movements and gestures help to bring out Antonio's mood? What might he be doing as this first scene opens, for example?

Themes and issues

- In what ways does the opening dialogue show that a primary concern of these characters is **money and business**?

1 **sooth**: truth
4 **whereof … born**: what has given rise to it
6 **want-wit**: senseless fool / idiot
7 **ado**: trouble
9 **argosies**: large merchant ships
   portly sail: full, majestic sails
10 **signiors**: gentlemen
   burghers: citizens
11 **pageants**: spectacular open-air shows
12 **overpeer**: look down on
   petty traffickers: inferior trading ships
13 **curtsy**: bow / bob up and down
   do them reverence: show them respect
14 **woven wings**: sails
15 **venture forth**: risky enterprises at sea
16 **affections**: thoughts and emotions
17 **hopes abroad**: prospects at sea
   still: always, constantly
18 **Plucking … wind**: dropping blades of grass to see which way the wind is blowing
19 **roads**: anchorages
23 **ague**: shivering fever
26 **flats**: sandbanks
27 **Andrew**: The name of a real ship, a famous Spanish galleon.
28 **Vailing**: bowing down
   her high top: the tops of her masts
   ribs: ribbed frame
29 **her burial**: the seabed where she is wrecked
30 **edifice**: building
31 **bethink me straight**: immediately think about
32 **touching but**: merely touching

A street in Venice.

Enter ANTONIO, SALERIO, *and* SOLANIO.

ANTONIO	In sooth, I know not why I am so sad.
	It wearies me – you say it wearies you –
	But how I caught it, found it, or came by it,
	What stuff 'tis made of, whereof it is born,
	I am to learn. 5
	And such a want-wit sadness makes of me
	That I have much ado to know myself.
SALERIO	Your mind is tossing on the ocean –
	There where your argosies with portly sail,
	Like signiors and rich burghers on the flood, 10
	Or as it were the pageants of the sea,
	Do overpeer the petty traffickers
	That curtsy to them, do them reverence,
	As they fly by them with their woven wings.
SOLANIO	Believe me, sir, had I such venture forth, 15
	The better part of my affections would
	Be with my hopes abroad. I should be still
	Plucking the grass to know where sits the wind,
	Peering in maps for ports, and piers, and roads –
	And every object that might make me fear 20
	Misfortune to my venture, out of doubt
	Would make me sad.
SALERIO	My wind, cooling my broth,
	Would blow me to an ague when I thought
	What harm a wind too great might do at sea.
	I should not see the sandy hour-glass run 25
	But I should think of shallows and of flats,
	And see my wealthy Andrew docked in sand,
	Vailing her high top lower than her ribs
	To kiss her burial. Should I go to church
	And see the holy edifice of stone 30
	And not bethink me straight of dangerous rocks,
	Which touching but my gentle vessel's side

Antonio denies that he is concerned about his cargoes, or that he is in love. Salerio and Solanio leave when Antonio's other friends, Bassanio, Gratiano and Lorenzo, arrive.

33 **stream**: current
34 **Enrobe**: dress up
35 **but even now**: only just now

38 **bechanced**: if it happened

42 **in one bottom trusted**: invested all in one ship's hold
43 **estate**: fortune
44 **Upon**: dependent upon

46 **Fie, fie!**: Rubbish!

50 **Janus**: the Roman god with two faces
51 **framed**: created
52 **peep**: squint while laughing
53 **bagpiper**: Bagpipes were thought to make a gloomy sound.
54 **other**: others
   vinegar aspect: sour looks
56 **though Nestor … laughable**: even though someone as old and grave as Nestor (a hero in Greek myth) swore it was funny

61 **prevented me**: got in first

64 **embrace th' occasion**: welcome the opportunity

THINK ABOUT for GCSE

Performance and staging

• What reasons do Salerio and Solanio suggest for Antonio's 'sadness'? In what very different ways might an actor deliver Antonio's response 'Fie, fie!' (line 46) and what meaning would each one convey to the audience?

Characterisation

• What are your initial impressions of Salerio and Solanio? What main purposes do they serve at the beginning of the play?

	Would scatter all her spices on the stream,	
	Enrobe the roaring waters with my silks,	
	And, in a word, but even now worth this,	35
	And now worth nothing? Shall I have the thought	
	To think on this, and shall I lack the thought	
	That such a thing bechanced would make me sad?	
	But tell not me: I know Antonio	
	Is sad to think upon his merchandise.	40
ANTONIO	Believe me, no. I thank my fortune for it,	
	My ventures are not in one bottom trusted,	
	Nor to one place – nor is my whole estate	
	Upon the fortune of this present year.	
	Therefore my merchandise makes me not sad.	45
SOLANIO	Why then, you are in love.	
ANTONIO	Fie, fie!	
SOLANIO	Not in love neither? Then let us say you are sad	
	Because you are not merry – and 'twere as easy	
	For you to laugh and leap, and say you are merry	
	Because you are not sad. Now, by two-headed Janus,	50
	Nature hath framed strange fellows in her time:	
	Some that will evermore peep through their eyes	
	And laugh like parrots at a bagpiper –	
	And other of such vinegar aspect	
	That they'll not show their teeth in way of smile	55
	Though Nestor swear the jest be laughable.	

Enter BASSANIO, LORENZO, *and* GRATIANO.

	– Here comes Bassanio, your most noble kinsman,	
	Gratiano, and Lorenzo. Fare ye well –	
	We leave you now with better company.	
SALERIO	I would have stayed till I had made you merry,	60
	If worthier friends had not prevented me.	
ANTONIO	Your worth is very dear in my regard.	
	I take it your own business calls on you,	
	And you embrace th' occasion to depart.	
SALERIO	Good morrow, my good lords.	65

Gratiano attempts to cheer
Antonio up and advises him not
to behave seriously all the time
in an attempt to appear wise.

THINK ABOUT for GCSE

Relationships

• What do we learn from
lines 57 to 68? Why might
Solanio and Salerio say
that Bassanio, Gratiano
and Lorenzo are 'better
company' and 'worthier
friends' (lines 59 and 61)?
How genuine is Antonio's
reassurance (lines 62 to 64)?
What lies behind Bassanio's
question and Salerio's
response (lines 66 to 68)?

Context

• In Shakespeare's time, the
world was often compared
to the theatre: the motto
of Shakespeare's Globe
playhouse is thought to have
been 'All the world plays
the actor'. How helpful is
Antonio's comment (lines 77
to 79) in shedding light on
his personality?

66 **laugh**: meet up and have some fun
67 **grow exceeding strange**: have become
very distant / like a stranger
68 **We'll … yours**: We'll ensure we are free
when you are

74 **You … world**: You take everything too
seriously
75 **They … care**: people who worry too
much lose the enjoyment of life
76 **marvellously**: extremely / amazingly
77 **hold**: consider
81 **liver**: The liver was believed to be the
source of lust and other passions.
82 **mortifying**: deadly (Groans and sighs
were thought to drain blood from the
heart.)
84 **his … alabaster**: a stone monument to
his ancestor
85 **creep … jaundice**: grow depressed and
bitter
86 **peevish**: bad-tempered
88 **visages**: faces
89 **cream and mantle**: become scummed
over
standing: stagnant
90 **wilful**: deliberate
entertain: maintain
91–2 **dressed … of**: given a reputation for
92 **conceit**: understanding
93 **As … say**: as if to say
Sir Oracle: 'The Wise One' (An
oracle was a source of wisdom and
prophecies.)
96 **reputed**: said to be
98–9 **would … fools**: people would call them
a fool and (according to the Bible) might
be damned for doing so

BASSANIO	Good signiors both, when shall we laugh? – Say, when?
	You grow exceeding strange. Must it be so?
SALERIO	We'll make our leisures to attend on yours.

Exit, with SOLANIO.

LORENZO	My Lord Bassanio, since you have found Antonio
	We two will leave you, but at dinner-time 70
	I pray you have in mind where we must meet.
BASSANIO	I will not fail you.
GRATIANO	You look not well, Signior Antonio.
	You have too much respect upon the world:
	They lose it that do buy it with much care. 75
	Believe me, you are marvellously changed.
ANTONIO	I hold the world but as the world, Gratiano –
	A stage where every man must play a part,
	And mine a sad one.
GRATIANO	Let me play the fool!
	With mirth and laughter let old wrinkles come, 80
	And let my liver rather heat with wine
	Than my heart cool with mortifying groans.
	Why should a man whose blood is warm within
	Sit like his grandsire, cut in alabaster?
	Sleep when he wakes? – And creep into the jaundice 85
	By being peevish? I tell thee what, Antonio –
	I love thee, and 'tis my love that speaks –
	There are a sort of men whose visages
	Do cream and mantle like a standing pond,
	And do a wilful stillness entertain, 90
	With purpose to be dressed in an opinion
	Of wisdom, gravity, profound conceit –
	As who should say, 'I am Sir Oracle,
	And when I ope my lips, let no dog bark!'
	O my Antonio, I do know of these 95
	That therefore only are reputed wise
	For saying nothing – when I am very sure,
	If they should speak, would almost damn those ears
	Which, hearing them, would call their brothers fools.
	I'll tell thee more of this another time – 100

Antonio asks Bassanio the identity of the lady he had promised to tell him about. Bassanio reminds Antonio that he owes money to a lot of people, Antonio most of all.

101–2 But … opinion: don't use melancholy to lure people into giving you a reputation for being wise

102 gudgeon: small, worthless fish

104 exhortation: earnest speech / sermon

110 I'll grow … gear: all this will turn me into a talker

111 commendable: praiseworthy

112 neat's: ox's
vendible: saleable, marketable (i.e. too old or poor to get married)

113 Is that anything now?: What was that all about?

115 reasons: sensible statements
as: like

116 two … chaff: a great pile of husks

117 ere: before

THINK ABOUT for GCSE

Characterisation

- Bassanio observes that Gratiano 'speaks an infinite deal of nothing' (line 114). What impression have you formed of Gratiano?

Relationships

- What does Antonio's question (lines 119 to 121) suggest about a previous conversation and Bassanio's relationship with Antonio?

Language

- What do we learn about Bassanio's background from his use of language here? Think particularly about 'disabled mine estate' (line 123), 'a more swelling port' (line 124), and 'something too prodigal' (line 129).

123 disabled mine estate: seriously reduced my wealth / depleted my fortune

124 something: to some extent
swelling port: extravagant lifestyle

125 faint: inadequate
grant continuance: allow me to keep up

126–7 abridged from: deprived of

127 noble rate: expensive lifestyle
care: concern

128 come … from: find an honourable way out of

129 time … prodigal: rather wasteful past

130 gaged: owing / committed

132 warranty: authorisation / permission

133 unburden: reveal to you

But fish not with this melancholy bait
For this fool gudgeon, this opinion.
Come, good Lorenzo. – Fare ye well a while.
I'll end my exhortation after dinner.

LORENZO Well, we will leave you then till dinner-time. 105
I must be one of these same dumb wise men,
For Gratiano never lets me speak.

GRATIANO Well, keep me company but two years more,
Thou shalt not know the sound of thine own tongue.

ANTONIO Fare you well – I'll grow a talker for this gear. 110

GRATIANO Thanks i' faith – for silence is only commendable
In a neat's tongue dried and a maid not vendible.

Exit, with LORENZO.

ANTONIO Is that anything now?

BASSANIO Gratiano speaks an infinite deal of nothing – more than
any man in all Venice. His reasons are as two grains of 115
wheat hid in two bushels of chaff: you shall seek all day
ere you find them, and when you have them they are
not worth the search.

ANTONIO Well, tell me now what lady is the same
To whom you swore a secret pilgrimage, 120
That you today promised to tell me of.

BASSANIO 'Tis not unknown to you, Antonio,
How much I have disabled mine estate
By something showing a more swelling port
Than my faint means would grant continuance. 125
Nor do I now make moan to be abridged
From such a noble rate – but my chief care
Is to come fairly off from the great debts
Wherein my time, something too prodigal,
Hath left me gaged. To you, Antonio, 130
I owe the most in money and in love,
And from your love I have a warranty
To unburden all my plots and purposes
How to get clear of all the debts I owe.

Bassanio explains the plan that will enable him to pay off all his debts and tells Antonio about Portia, a wealthy heiress who lives in Belmont. Bassanio explains that famous men come from all parts of the world in the hope of marrying her.

THINK ABOUT for GCSE

Characterisation

- In Bassanio's first reference to Portia (lines 161 to 163) he describes her as rich, beautiful and virtuous. From your impression of him so far, do you think that this is his order of priorities?

Language

- In describing Portia and her many suitors, Bassanio recalls the myth of Jason and the quest for the Golden Fleece (lines 168 to 172). What does this suggest about the suitors' motives in wanting to marry Portia?

136–7 **And if ... honour**: if this plan is as honourable as you yourself have always been
138 **my extremest means**: anything I have or can possibly do
139 **occasions**: needs
140 **shaft**: arrow
141 **flight**: type
142 **advisèd**: deliberate / careful
143 **forth**: out
adventuring: risking
144 **oft**: often
urge: put forward
proof: experience
145 **innocence**: simple sincerity
146 **wilful**: headstrong / impetuous
148 **self**: same
150–1 **or ... Or**: either ... or
151 **your latter hazard**: the second one risked
152 **rest debtor**: remain in your debt
153 **herein ... time**: now you are only wasting time
154 **wind ... circumstance**: go in a roundabout way to use my affection for you
155 **out of doubt**: certainly
156 **making ... uttermost**: doubting that I will give you all I have
160 **prest unto it**: ready / driven to do it
161 **richly left**: who has been left a fortune
163 **Sometimes**: Once
165–6 **nothing undervalued to**: worth no less than
166 **Cato's ... Portia**: Brutus's wife who appears in Shakespeare's *Julius Caesar*.
169 **Renownèd suitors**: famous men who want to marry her
sunny locks: shining blonde hair
171 **seat**: country estate
strand: shore
171–2 **Colchos' ... Jasons**: In mythology, the hero Jason and his Argonauts quested for the Golden Fleece in Colchis.

ANTONIO	I pray you, good Bassanio, let me know it –	135
	And if it stand, as you yourself still do,	
	Within the eye of honour, be assured	
	My purse, my person, my extremest means	
	Lie all unlocked to your occasions.	

BASSANIO	In my school-days, when I had lost one shaft,	140
	I shot his fellow of the self-same flight	
	The self-same way, with more advisèd watch	
	To find the other forth, and by adventuring both	
	I oft found both. I urge this childhood proof	
	Because what follows is pure innocence.	145
	I owe you much, and like a wilful youth	
	That which I owe is lost. But if you please	
	To shoot another arrow that self way	
	Which you did shoot the first, I do not doubt,	
	As I will watch the aim, or to find both	150
	Or bring your latter hazard back again,	
	And thankfully rest debtor for the first.	

ANTONIO	You know me well, and herein spend but time	
	To wind about my love with circumstance.	
	And out of doubt you do me now more wrong	155
	In making question of my uttermost	
	Than if you had made waste of all I have.	
	Then do but say to me what I should do	
	That in your knowledge may by me be done,	
	And I am prest unto it: therefore speak.	160

BASSANIO	In Belmont is a lady richly left,	
	And she is fair, and – fairer than that word –	
	Of wondrous virtues. Sometimes from her eyes	
	I did receive fair speechless messages.	
	Her name is Portia, nothing undervalued	165
	To Cato's daughter, Brutus' Portia.	
	Nor is the wide world ignorant of her worth –	
	For the four winds blow in from every coast	
	Renownèd suitors, and her sunny locks	
	Hang on her temples like a golden fleece,	170
	Which makes her seat of Belmont Colchos' strand,	
	And many Jasons come in quest of her.	
	O my Antonio, had I but the means	

Bassanio reveals his intention to woo Portia himself. Antonio explains that, as all his cash is tied up in investments, he will need to borrow the money Bassanio needs to finance his visit to Portia.

175 **presages**: that predicts
thrift: profit / success
176 **questionless**: undoubtedly / without question
178 **commodity**: goods
179 **a present sum**: the ready money
180 **Try ... do**: see what you can borrow in my name
181 **racked ... uttermost**: stretched to its limits
182 **furnish thee**: equip you to go
183 **presently**: immediately
184 **no question make**: have no doubt
185 **of my trust**: on my credit (i.e. as a business deal)
for my sake: as an act of friendship / because I am known personally

THINK ABOUT for GCSE

Themes and issues

- **Money and business**: How much of the opening scene has established that this is a society concerned with business, money and merchandise? Look back, for example, at lines 15, 40 to 45, 112, 123 to 134, 138, 152, 161, 175, and 178 to 185.

Characterisation

- What impression have you formed of Bassanio from this opening scene?

Themes and issues

- **Love and friendship**: How would you describe the nature of Antonio's friendship with Bassanio? What do we learn from Antonio's offer (lines 177 to 185)?

	To hold a rival place with one of them,	
	I have a mind presages me such thrift	**175**
	That I should questionless be fortunate.	

ANTONIO   Thou know'st that all my fortunes are at sea –
Neither have I money nor commodity
To raise a present sum. Therefore go forth –
Try what my credit can in Venice do,   **180**
That shall be racked even to the uttermost
To furnish thee to Belmont to fair Portia.
Go presently inquire, and so will I,
Where money is – and I no question make
To have it of my trust, or for my sake.   **185**

Exit, with BASSANIO.

In this scene ...

- Portia and Nerissa discuss the suitors for Portia's hand in marriage.
- They hear that another suitor, the Prince of Morocco, is on his way.

Portia is depressed because the will left by her dead father prevents her from choosing a husband. Instead, any man who wants to marry her has to pick one of three caskets – gold, silver or lead. Whoever chooses the right one will become her husband.

THINK ABOUT for GCSE

Structure and form

- What similarity do you notice between the openings of Scenes 1 and 2? What is the effect of this echo?

Characterisation

- To what extent is Portia's life influenced by her dead father?

Themes and issues

- **Love and friendship**: How does Nerissa justify the 'lottery' of the caskets imposed by Portia's father's will (lines 26 to 31)?

1	**troth**: faith (i.e. I swear)
3	**would be**: would have good reason to be
5	**aught**: anything
	surfeit: overeat
7	**mean**: small / limited
7–8	**seated in the mean**: 1 situated in the middle; 2 having neither too much nor too little
8	**superfluity**: eating and drinking too much
	comes … hairs: makes you older sooner
9	**competency**: having just enough
10	**sentences**: wise sayings
	pronounced: delivered / spoken
13	**had been**: would have been
14	**divine**: clergyman / preacher
17	**devise laws**: create rules
17–18	**for the blood**: to govern our passions
18	**hot temper**: passionate temperament
	cold decree: sensible advice
19	**meshes**: nets / traps
20	**counsel**: advice
22	**would**: want
23	**curbed**: restrained / held in check
24	**will**: 1 wishes; 2 will (in the legal sense)
27	**inspirations**: ideas
	lottery: game of chance
29	**whereof**: in which
	who … meaning: whoever chooses the chest your father intended
30–1	**rightly … rightly**: correctly … truly
32	**affection**: inclinations / feelings

Belmont: Portia's house.

Enter PORTIA, *with her waiting-woman* NERISSA.

PORTIA   By my troth, Nerissa, my little body is aweary of
              this great world.

NERISSA   You would be, sweet madam, if your miseries were
              in the same abundance as your good fortunes are –
              and yet for aught I see, they are as sick that surfeit   5
              with too much, as they that starve with nothing. It
              is no mean happiness therefore to be seated in the
              mean – superfluity comes sooner by white hairs, but
              competency lives longer.

PORTIA   Good sentences, and well pronounced.   10

NERISSA   They would be better if well followed.

PORTIA   If to do were as easy as to know what were good to do,
              chapels had been churches, and poor men's cottages
              princes' palaces. It is a good divine that follows his
              own instructions. I can easier teach twenty what were   15
              good to be done than be one of the twenty to follow
              mine own teaching. The brain may devise laws for the
              blood, but a hot temper leaps o'er a cold decree – such
              a hare is madness the youth, to skip o'er the meshes of
              good counsel the cripple. But this reasoning is not in   20
              the fashion to choose me a husband. O me, the word
              'choose'! I may neither choose who I would, nor refuse
              who I dislike – so is the will of a living daughter curbed
              by the will of a dead father. Is it not hard, Nerissa, that
              I cannot choose one, nor refuse none?   25

NERISSA   Your father was ever virtuous, and holy men at their
              death have good inspirations. Therefore the lottery that
              he hath devised in these three chests, of gold, silver, and
              lead, whereof who chooses his meaning chooses you,
              will no doubt never be chosen by any rightly but one   30
              who you shall rightly love. But what warmth is there in
              your affection towards any of these princely suitors that
              are already come?

Nerissa lists the current group of suitors and Portia speaks mockingly about each one.

THINK ABOUT for **GCSE**

Performance and staging

- Portia asks Nerissa to name the suitors so that she can comment on them. In what interesting and amusing ways might the dialogue that follows be performed?

Context

- Shakespeare occasionally mocks his own countrymen in his plays. What particular jokes is he making about the English in Portia's comments on Falconbridge (lines 63 to 70)?

34 **over-name**: list
36 **level at**: guess at / work out
37 **Neapolitan**: from Naples in Italy
38 **colt**: 1 young horse; 2 immature boy
39 **appropriation to**: special feature of
40 **good parts**: talents
41 **played false**: was unfaithful
42 **smith**: blacksmith
43 **County Palatine**: Count (regional nobleman) with royal powers
44 **as who should**: like a person who would
    An: If
45 **choose**: please yourself
46 **the weeping philosopher**: The Greek Heraclitus, who wept at people's foolishness.
47 **unmannerly**: 1 impolite; 2 inappropriate (because he is young)
    sadness: melancholy / depression
48 **death's-head**: skull
51 **How say you by**: What do you think of
55–6 **he is … no man**: he imitates everyone and has no character of his own
56 **throstle**: song thrush
56–7 **falls … capering**: immediately starts dancing about
59 **for if**: even if
60 **requite him**: return his love

64 **hath neither**: does not speak
66 **poor pennyworth**: very small amount
66–7 **is a … picture**: looks like a handsome man
68 **dumb-show**: play in mime
    suited: dressed
69 **doublet**: close-fitting jacket
    round hose: stockings and padded breeches
70 **bonnet**: hat

PORTIA	I pray thee over-name them, and as thou namest them I will describe them – and according to my description level at my affection.

35

NERISSA	First there is the Neapolitan prince.

PORTIA	Ay, that's a colt indeed, for he doth nothing but talk of his horse – and he makes it a great appropriation to his own good parts that he can shoe him himself. I am much afeared my lady his mother played false with a smith.

40

NERISSA	Then is there the County Palatine.

PORTIA	He doth nothing but frown – as who should say 'An you will not have me, choose.' He hears merry tales and smiles not. I fear he will prove the weeping philosopher when he grows old, being so full of unmannerly sadness in his youth. I had rather be married to a death's-head with a bone in his mouth than to either of these. God defend me from these two!

45

50

NERISSA	How say you by the French lord, Monsieur Le Bon?

PORTIA	God made him, and therefore let him pass for a man. In truth I know it is a sin to be a mocker, but he! – Why, he hath a horse better than the Neapolitan's, a better bad habit of frowning than the Count Palatine: he is every man in no man. If a throstle sing, he falls straight a-capering. He will fence with his own shadow. If I should marry him, I should marry twenty husbands. If he would despise me, I would forgive him – for if he love me to madness, I shall never requite him.

55

60

NERISSA	What say you then to Falconbridge, the young baron of England?

PORTIA	You know I say nothing to him – for he understands not me, nor I him. He hath neither Latin, French, nor Italian – and you will come into the court and swear that I have a poor pennyworth in the English. He is a proper man's picture – but alas! – Who can converse with a dumb-show? How oddly he is suited! I think he bought his doublet in Italy, his round hose in France, his bonnet in Germany, and his behaviour everywhere.

65

70

Nerissa reveals that all the suitors they have been discussing have decided to pull out of the contest and return home.

72 **charity**: friendship
73 **borrowed**: 1 received; 2 took as a loan
74 **again**: back
75 **surety**: promised to pay the debt if the Scotsman was unable
    sealed under: set his seal (i.e. signed a pledge)
75–6 **for another**: to receive another smack

82–3 **An ... fell**: If the worst thing that could ever happen, does happen
83 **make shift**: manage

85 **offer**: attempt
86 **you should**: you would

THINK ABOUT for GCSE

Performance and staging

• Nerissa has known all along that the suitors on her list have decided not to take part in the 'lottery' of the caskets. In what different ways might Portia react when Nerissa tells her (lines 93 to 98)?

Language

• How do the classical references in lines 99 to 101 help to convey the strength of Portia's vow concerning her father's will?

89 **Rhenish**: from the Rhineland (Germany)
    contrary: wrong
90 **without**: on the outside
91 **ere**: before
92 **sponge**: heavy drinker
94 **acquainted me with**: informed me of
    determinations: decisions / resolutions
96 **suit**: courtship
97 **sort**: way / method
    imposition: command (i.e. in his will)

99 **Sibylla**: A Greek prophetess who was granted long life by Apollo.
100 **Diana**: goddess of virginity
101 **parcel**: bunch
102 **dote on**: love excessively

105 **hither**: here

NERISSA	What think you of the Scottish lord, his neighbour?
PORTIA	That he hath a neighbourly charity in him – for he borrowed a box of the ear of the Englishman, and swore he would pay him again when he was able. I think the Frenchman became his surety, and sealed under for another.

75

NERISSA	How like you the young German, the Duke of Saxony's nephew?
PORTIA	Very vilely in the morning when he is sober, and *most* vilely in the afternoon when he is drunk! When he is best he is a little worse than a man, and when he is worst he is little better than a beast. An the worst fall that ever fell, I hope I shall make shift to go without him.

80

NERISSA	If he should offer to choose – and choose the right casket – you should refuse to perform your father's will if you should refuse to accept him.

85

PORTIA	Therefore, for fear of the worst, I pray thee set a deep glass of Rhenish wine on the contrary casket – for if the devil be within, and that temptation without, I know he will choose it. I will do anything, Nerissa, ere I will be married to a sponge.

90

NERISSA	You need not fear, lady, the having any of these lords. They have acquainted me with their determinations, which is indeed to return to their home, and to trouble you with no more suit – unless you may be won by some other sort than your father's imposition, depending on the caskets.

95

PORTIA	If I live to be as old as Sibylla, I will die as chaste as Diana unless I be obtained by the manner of my father's will. I am glad this parcel of wooers are so reasonable, for there is not one among them but I dote on his very absence. And I pray God grant them a fair departure.

100

NERISSA	Do you not remember, lady, in your father's time, a Venetian, a scholar and a soldier, that came hither in company of the Marquis of Montferrat?

105

Portia has fond memories of a young Venetian, called Bassanio, who once visited Belmont. She is not pleased to hear that a new suitor, the Prince of Morocco, is on his way.

108 **foolish**: inexperienced

113–4 **four strangers … fifth**: Nerissa has already listed six. Perhaps Shakespeare forgot.

114 **forerunner**: messenger

119 **condition**: character
120 **complexion**: 1 skin colouring; 2 temperament
    devil: Devils were traditionally black.
    shrive me: hear me confess my sins (like a priest)
121 **wive**: marry
122 **Sirrah**: Sir (a way of addressing male servants: 'You there!')

THINK ABOUT for GCSE

Performance and staging

- What is Portia's reaction to Nerissa's reference to 'a scholar and a soldier' (lines 104 to 106) who once visited Portia's father? How might Portia say line 107 and lines 110 to 111?

Themes and issues

- **Hatred and prejudice**: Portia's reaction to hearing about the Prince of Morocco (lines 119 to 121) may strike modern audiences as racist. How do you react to it?

Characterisation

- What impression have you formed of Portia from this scene?

PORTIA   Yes, yes, it was Bassanio! – as I think so was he called.

NERISSA   True, madam – he of all the men that ever my foolish eyes looked upon was the best deserving a fair lady.

PORTIA   I remember him well, and I remember him worthy of   **110**
thy praise.

Enter a SERVANT.

– How now? What news?

SERVANT   The four strangers seek for you, madam, to take their leave – and there is a forerunner come from a fifth, the Prince of Morocco, who brings word the prince his   **115**
master will he here tonight.

PORTIA   If I could bid the fifth welcome with so good heart as I can bid the other four farewell, I should be glad of his approach. If he have the condition of a saint and the complexion of a devil, I had rather he should shrive me   **120**
than wive me.

Come, Nerissa. (*To the* SERVANT) Sirrah, go before.

Exit SERVANT.

Whiles we shut the gate upon one wooer, another
knocks at the door.

Exit, with NERISSA.

In this scene ...

- After an angry conversation between Shylock and Antonio, Shylock agrees to lend Antonio the money he needs. Shylock will charge no interest but instead can take a pound of Antonio's flesh if Antonio fails to repay the sum on the due date.

1 **ducats**: gold coins

Bassanio approaches the money-lender, Shylock, for a loan of three thousand ducats. Despite expressing concern about the security of Antonio's investments, Shylock seems willing to lend him the money.

4 **bound**: legally responsible for repaying the loan
6 **stead**: help
pleasure: oblige

THINK ABOUT for GCSE

Language

- What have Bassanio and Shylock been discussing as the scene opens? What do Shylock's opening responses (lines 1 to 11) suggest about his reaction to their conversation?

Themes and issues

- **Money and business**: What aspect of finance in Venice is explored in this exchange between Shylock and Bassanio?

12 **imputation**: suggestion / accusation
14 **he is sufficient**: he has enough money (i.e. to repay the loan)
15 **his ... supposition**: there are doubts about his finances
argosy: merchant ship
16 **Tripolis**: Tripoli (now in Libya)
Indies: East Indies
17 **the Rialto**: the merchants' business centre in Venice (district with the famous bridge)
19 **squandered**: scattered (perhaps recklessly)
23 **notwithstanding**: despite all that
24 **take his bond**: accept the agreement, with Antonio responsible for the loan
25 **assured**: reassured
26 **be assured**: obtain guarantees / make sure
27 **bethink me**: consider

Act 1 Scene 3

Venice.

***Enter* Bassanio *and* Shylock.**

Shylock	Three thousand ducats – well.
Bassanio	Ay sir, for three months.
Shylock	For three months – well.
Bassanio	For the which, as I told you, Antonio shall be bound.
Shylock	Antonio shall become bound – well.

5

Bassanio	May you stead me? Will you pleasure me? – Shall I know your answer?
Shylock	Three thousand ducats – for three months, and Antonio bound.
Bassanio	Your answer to that?

10

Shylock	Antonio is a good man.
Bassanio	Have you heard any imputation to the contrary?
Shylock	O no – no, no, no. My meaning in saying he is a good man is to have you understand me that he is sufficient. Yet his means are in supposition: he hath an argosy bound to Tripolis, another to the Indies. I understand, moreover, upon the Rialto, he hath a third at Mexico, a fourth for England, and other ventures he hath squandered abroad. But ships are but boards, sailors but men: there be land-rats and water-rats, water-thieves and land-thieves – I mean pirates – and then there is the peril of waters, winds, and rocks. The man is, notwithstanding, sufficient. Three thousand ducats – I think I may take his bond.

15

20

Bassanio	Be assured you may.

25

Shylock	I *will* be assured I may – and that I may be assured, I will bethink me. May I speak with Antonio?
Bassanio	If it please you to dine with us.

When Antonio arrives, Shylock tells the audience how much he hates him and why, vowing to get his revenge if he can. Shylock tells Antonio that a fellow Jew, Tubal, will provide the money that Antonio wants to borrow.

THINK ABOUT for GCSE

Characterisation

- Bassanio invites Shylock to dine with him and Antonio. What do we learn from Shylock's response (lines 29 to 33) about his religion and his attitude to its laws?

- Shylock's aside (lines 36 to 47) is very important in understanding both his character and his subsequent behaviour. What reasons does he give for hating Antonio and what does he hope to do given the chance?

Themes and issues

- **Hatred and prejudice**: In what ways does Shylock's aside introduce the play's treatment of social/racial prejudice?

29 **pork**: Jews are forbidden to eat pork.
29–30 **to eat … into**: Shylock refers to the story in the Bible where Jesus made devils enter the bodies of pigs.

36 **fawning**: excessively flattering / obsequious
publican: tax-collector (In Biblical times, Roman tax-gatherers oppressed Jews.)
37 **for**: because
38 **for that**: because
low simplicity: base naivety / foolish humility
39 **gratis**: free (i.e. without charging interest)
40 **rate of usance**: interest rate
41 **catch … hip**: (a wrestling term) once get him at my mercy
42 **feed fat**: satisfy to the full
43 **our sacred nation**: the Jewish people
43–5 **rails … on me**: is abusive about
45 **thrift**: money acquired by careful management
48 **debating … store**: considering how much ready money I have
50 **gross**: full amount
52 **Hebrew**: Jew
53 **furnish**: supply
soft!: wait a minute!
54 **Rest you fair**: May you remain well (i.e. Good health to you!)
55 **in our mouths**: that we were speaking of
56 **albeit**: although
57 **excess**: interest
58 **ripe wants**: pressing needs
59 **Is he yet possessed**: Has he been told
60 **ye would**: you want

SHYLOCK	Yes – to smell pork, to eat of the habitation which your prophet the Nazarite conjured the devil into. I will buy **30** with you, sell with you, talk with you, walk with you, and so following – but I will not eat with you, drink with you, nor pray with you.

Enter ANTONIO.

                      – What news on the Rialto? Who is he comes here?

BASSANIO   This is Signior Antonio.   **35**

SHYLOCK   (*Aside*) How like a fawning publican he looks!
                      I hate him for he is a Christian –
                      But more, for that in low simplicity
                      He lends out money gratis, and brings down
                      The rate of usance here with us in Venice.   **40**
                      If I can catch him once upon the hip,
                      I will feed fat the ancient grudge I bear him.
                      He hates our sacred nation, and he rails,
                      Even there where merchants most do congregate,
                      On me, my bargains, and my well-won thrift,   **45**
                      Which he calls interest. Cursed be my tribe
                      If I forgive him!

BASSANIO   Shylock, do you hear?

SHYLOCK   I am debating of my present store,
                      And by the near guess of my memory
                      I cannot instantly raise up the gross   **50**
                      Of full three thousand ducats. What of that?
                      Tubal, a wealthy Hebrew of my tribe,
                      Will furnish me. But soft! – how many months
                      Do you desire? (*To* ANTONIO) Rest you fair, good
                          signior –
                      Your worship was the last man in our mouths.   **55**

ANTONIO   Shylock, albeit I neither lend nor borrow
                      By taking nor by giving of excess,
                      Yet to supply the ripe wants of my friend,
                      I'll break a custom. (*To* BASSANIO) Is he yet possessed
                      How much ye would?

SHYLOCK   Ay, ay – three thousand ducats.   **60**

Antonio tells Shylock that he disapproves of charging interest. To support his view that interest is acceptable, Shylock tells the story of Jacob and Laban in the Bible.

THINK ABOUT for GCSE

Themes and issues

- **Money and business**: What point is Shylock trying to make, in telling the story of Jacob and Laban (lines 66 to 85)?

Characterisation

- Many actors have brought out the humour in Shylock. What potential has there been for comedy so far in this scene? Think about the situation, Shylock's quick-wittedness, his sharp replies and vocal mannerisms.

64   **Methoughts**: It seemed to me

65   **Upon advantage**: where interest is involved

66   **Jacob ... Laban's**: The story of Jacob and his uncle Laban is in the Bible.

67   **Abram**: Abraham

68   **wrought in his behalf**: brought it about for his benefit

69   **third possessor**: (i.e. of the 'birthright')

72   **Mark**: Take note of

73   **were compromised**: had come to an agreement

74   **eanlings**: new-born lambs
     pied: of more than one colour

75   **fall as**: become
     hire: wages
     rank: on heat (i.e. ready to breed)

76   **turnèd to**: mated with

77   **work of generation**: act of mating

79   **pilled ... wands**: peeled strips of bark off some sticks

80   **in the ... kind**: during the natural act (i.e. of mating)

81   **fulsome**: lustful

82–3   **Who ... lambs**: An offspring's nature was thought to depend on what its mother was looking at when they were conceived.

82   **eaning**: lambing

83   **Fall**: give birth to
     parti-coloured: of more than one colour

84   **thrive**: profit

86   **venture**: enterprise
     served: worked

88   **swayed and fashioned**: influenced and brought about

89   **inserted**: introduced
     good: justifiable

91   **I cannot tell**: I don't know about that

93   **cite scripture**: quote examples from the Bible (like **producing holy witness**, line 94)

ANTONIO	And for three months.
SHYLOCK	I had forgot – three months – (*To* BASSANIO) you told me so. Well then, your bond – and let me see – but hear you, Methoughts you said you neither lend nor borrow Upon advantage.
ANTONIO	I do never use it. **65**
SHYLOCK	When Jacob grazed his uncle Laban's sheep – This Jacob from our holy Abram was – As his wise mother wrought in his behalf – The third possessor – ay, he was the third –
ANTONIO	And what of him? Did he take interest? **70**
SHYLOCK	No, not take interest – not as you would say Directly interest. Mark what Jacob did: When Laban and himself were compromised That all the eanlings which were streaked and pied Should fall as Jacob's hire, the ewes being rank **75** In end of autumn turnèd to the rams. And when the work of generation was Between these woolly breeders in the act, The skilful shepherd pilled me certain wands, And in the doing of the deed of kind **80** He stuck them up before the fulsome ewes, Who then conceiving, did in eaning time Fall parti-coloured lambs – and those were Jacob's. This was a way to thrive, and he was blest – And thrift is blessing if men steal it not. **85**
ANTONIO	This was a venture, sir, that Jacob served for – A thing not in his power to bring to pass, But swayed and fashioned by the hand of heaven. Was this inserted to make interest good? Or is your gold and silver ewes and rams? **90**
SHYLOCK	I cannot tell, I make it breed as fast – But note me, signior –
ANTONIO	Mark you this, Bassanio – The devil can cite scripture for his purpose.

When Antonio accuses Shylock of being a hypocrite, Shylock reminds Antonio how badly the merchant has treated him in the past, but Antonio is not sorry.

96 **goodly**: wholesome-looking
99 **rate:** (of interest)

100 **beholding**: in debt

102 **rated**: berated / criticised
103 **usances**: money-lending activities
104 **Still**: Always
105 **sufferance**: forbearance / putting up with things
     badge: distinguishing mark
     our tribe: Jews
107 **gaberdine**: loose cloak
110 **Go to**: All right
112 **void your rheum**: spit
113 **foot**: kick
     spurn: turn away / kick out
     stranger cur: stray dog
114 **threshold**: doorway
     moneys ... suit: you are asking for money
118 **bondman's key**: slave's tone of voice
119 **bated**: soft / subdued

THINK ABOUT *for* GCSE

Themes and issues

• In what ways does Antonio's response to Shylock's Bible story (lines 92 to 97) contribute to the play's treatment of **truth and deception**?

• **Hatred and prejudice:** What does Shylock say to Antonio (lines 101 to 124) that shows the ways that Christians sometimes insulted and oppressed Jews in Shakespeare's time?

Performance and staging

• What advice would you give to an actor on how to deliver Shylock's lines 101 to 124 most effectively? Think about the structure of the speech and the varying tone.

125 **like**: likely
129 **a breed for**: offspring of
     barren: unable to reproduce
     of: from
131 **break**: breaks the contract
     with better face: more cheerfully

	An evil soul producing holy witness	
	Is like a villain with a smiling cheek,	95
	A goodly apple rotten at the heart.	
	O what a goodly outside falsehood hath!	

SHYLOCK   Three thousand ducats – 'tis a good round sum.
           Three months from twelve – then let me see the rate –

ANTONIO   Well, Shylock, shall we be beholding to you?   100

SHYLOCK   Signior Antonio, many a time and oft
           In the Rialto you have rated me
           About my moneys and my usances.
           Still have I borne it with a patient shrug,
           For sufferance is the badge of all our tribe.   105
           You call me misbeliever, cut-throat dog,
           And spit upon my Jewish gaberdine –
           And all for use of that which is mine own.
           Well then, it now appears you need my help.
           Go to, then – you come to me, and you say,   110
           'Shylock, we would have moneys.' – You say so –
           You that did void your rheum upon my beard,
           And foot me as you spurn a stranger cur
           Over your threshold – moneys is your suit.
           What should I say to you? Should I not say   115
           'Hath a dog money? Is it possible
           A cur can lend three thousand ducats?' – Or
           Shall I bend low, and in a bondman's key,
           With bated breath and whisp'ring humbleness
           Say this: 120
           'Fair sir, you spat on me on Wednesday last –
           You spurned me such a day – another time
           You called me dog – and for these courtesies
           I'll lend you thus much moneys'?

ANTONIO   I am as like to call thee so again –   125
           To spit on thee again, to spurn thee too.
           If thou wilt lend this money, lend it not
           As to thy friends – for when did friendship take
           A breed for barren metal of his friend?
           But lend it rather to thine enemy –   130
           Who if he break, thou mayst with better face

Shylock offers to lend Antonio the money and charge no interest. Instead, if Antonio fails to repay the sum on time, Shylock can have a pound of Antonio's flesh. Bassanio is uneasy about the terms, but Antonio agrees.

THINK ABOUT for GCSE

Context

• The Christian Church had once taught that it was wrong for money to 'breed' money (line 129). How convincingly does Antonio express his objection to taking interest (lines 125 to 132)?

Characterisation

• Why is Shylock offering the bond? In an attempt to trap Antonio and get even with him? In order to mock Antonio and humiliate him with the 'pound of flesh' clause? Genuinely, in the hope of gaining Antonio's friendship? Or sincerely, because he may be tired of all the past hatred?

132 **Exact**: take / enforce
133 **would**: would like to

135 **no doit**: not a penny
136 **usance**: interest
137 **kind**: the natural / kind thing to do
    were: would be

139 **notary**: lawyer
    Seal: Sign and seal
140 **single bond**: contract with no conditions attached
    in a merry sport: as a joke
143 **forfeit**: penalty
144 **nominated for**: named as
    equal: exact

150 **dwell**: remain
    in my necessity: in need (i.e. of the money)
151 **forfeit**: break the contract by being unable to repay the loan

158 **break his day**: miss the deadline (i.e. for repayment)
159 **exaction**: enforcement
    forfeiture: penalty
161 **so estimable**: to be regarded as highly

164 **adieu**: goodbye

Exact the penalty.

SHYLOCK   Why, look you how you storm!
I would be friends with you, and have your love,
Forget the shames that you have stained me with,
Supply your present wants, and take no doit   135
Of usance for my moneys, and you'll not hear me.
This is kind I offer.

BASSANIO   This were kindness.

SHYLOCK   This kindness will I show:
Go with me to a notary. Seal me there
Your single bond, and – in a merry sport –   140
If you repay me not on such a day,
In such a place, such sum or sums as are
Expressed in the condition, let the forfeit
Be nominated for an equal pound
Of your fair flesh, to be cut off and taken   145
In what part of your body pleaseth me.

ANTONIO   Content, in faith! I'll seal to such a bond –
And say there is much kindness in the Jew.

BASSANIO   You shall not seal to such a bond for me!
I'll rather dwell in my necessity.   150

ANTONIO   Why, fear not, man, I will not forfeit it.
Within these two months – that's a month before
This bond expires – I do expect return
Of thrice three times the value of this bond.

SHYLOCK   O father Abram, what these Christians are,   155
Whose own hard dealings teaches them suspect
The thoughts of others! Pray you, tell me this:
If he should break his day, what should I gain
By the exaction of the forfeiture?
A pound of man's flesh taken from a man   160
Is not so estimable, profitable neither,
As flesh of muttons, beefs, or goats. I say,
To buy his favour I extend this friendship.
If he will take it, so – if not, adieu –
And for my love I pray you wrong me not.   165

Antonio reassures Bassanio: his ships are expected back a month before the repayment date.

167 **forthwith**: immediately
168 **direction**: instructions
169 **purse**: bag up
    straight: straight away
170 **fearful**: worrying / anxiety-making
171 **unthrifty**: careless
    knave: servant
    presently: straight away
172 **Hie thee**: Make haste / Hurry
    gentle 1 kind; 2 a pun on 'gentile' (non-Jewish)

THINK ABOUT for GCSE

Characterisation

- Why do you think Shylock calls the agreement 'this merry bond'? Why does Antonio accept Shylock's offer so readily, when Bassanio seems so uneasy about it (lines 147 to 154 and 174 to 176)?

Structure and form

- Think about Antonio's exit speech (lines 175 to 176). What do you think could go wrong?

ANTONIO   Yes, Shylock, I will seal unto this bond.

SHYLOCK   Then meet me forthwith at the notary's.
Give him direction for this merry bond,
And I will go and purse the ducats straight –
See to my house, left in the fearful guard   **170**
Of an unthrifty knave – and presently
I'll be with you.

Exit.

ANTONIO   Hie thee, gentle Jew.
– The Hebrew will turn Christian. He grows kind.

BASSANIO   I like not fair terms and a villain's mind.

ANTONIO   Come on – in this there can be no dismay: **175**
My ships come home a month before the day.

Exit, with BASSANIO.

In this scene ...

• The next of Portia's suitors arrives at Belmont: the Prince of Morocco.

The Prince of Morocco introduces himself.

THINK ABOUT for GCSE

Language

• In Morocco's opening speech, what shows that he means 'do not dislike me because of the colour of my skin'? What is Portia's response? What does she say about appearances (lines 13 to 14)? How does she play with the word 'fair' (line 20)?

Characterisation

• What aspect of himself does Morocco focus on in his opening speech (lines 1 to 12)? What do his words suggest about the way people often view him? What impression do you form of him?

1 **Mislike**: Dislike / Suspect
  complexion: skin colour
2 **livery**: uniform
  burnished: bright like polished metal
3 **near bred**: closely related
4 **fairest**: 1 most beautiful; 2 fairest-skinned
5 **Phœbus**: the sun god
6 **make incision**: cut ourselves (i.e. to draw blood)
7 **reddest**: Red was a sign of courage and nobility.
8 **aspect**: appearance
9 **feared the valiant**: frightened brave men
10 **best-regarded**: most admired
  clime: land
11 **hue**: colour
14 **nice**: over-fussy / 'choosy'
  direction: guidance
15 **lottery ... destiny**: game of chance on which my fate depends
16 **Bars**: does not allow
17 **scanted**: restricted
18 **hedged**: confined
  wit: wisdom
18–19 **yield ... who**: give myself as a wife to the man who
20 **as fair**: as fair a chance (a play on 'fair-skinned')
24 **scimitar**: curved sword
25 **Sophy**: Emperor of Persia
26 **fields of**: battles against
  Sultan Solyman: The ruler of Turkey.

ACT 2   SCENE 1

Belmont: Portia's house.

Trumpets sound.

*Enter the PRINCE OF MOROCCO (**dark-skinned, in a white robe**) and followers, with PORTIA, followed by NERISSA and servants.*

MOROCCO Mislike me not for my complexion,
The shadowed livery of the burnished sun,
To whom I am a neighbour and near bred.
Bring me the fairest creature northward born,
Where Phœbus' fire scarce thaws the icicles,   5
And let us make incision for your love
To prove whose blood is reddest, his or mine.
I tell thee, lady, this aspect of mine
Hath feared the valiant. By my love I swear,
The best-regarded virgins of our clime   10
Have loved it too. I would not change this hue,
Except to steal your thoughts, my gentle queen.

PORTIA   In terms of choice I am not solely led
By nice direction of a maiden's eyes.
Besides, the lottery of my destiny   15
Bars me the right of voluntary choosing.
But if my father had not scanted me,
And hedged me by his wit to yield myself
His wife who wins me by that means I told you,
Yourself, renownèd Prince, then stood as fair   20
As any comer I have looked on yet
For my affection.

MOROCCO   Even for that I thank you.
Therefore I pray you lead me to the caskets
To try my fortune. By this scimitar,
That slew the Sophy and a Persian prince   25
That won three fields of Sultan Solyman,
I would o'er-stare the sternest eyes that look,
Outbrave the heart most daring on the earth,
Pluck the young sucking cubs from the she-bear –
Yea, mock the lion when he roars for prey,   30

Portia reminds Morocco that, if he chooses the wrong casket, he must never propose marriage to another woman. He agrees.

31 **alas the while**: sad to say (expression of regret)
32 **Hercules**: A Greek hero, famous for his strength (also called **Alcides**, line 35). **Lichas**: Hercules's servant
35 **rage**: own rashness

42 **be advised**: think about this carefully

45 **hazard**: decision involving chance

THINK ABOUT *for* **GCSE**

Performance and staging

• If you were directing a modern-dress production of *The Merchant of Venice*, what would you want Morocco to look like?

	To win thee, lady. But alas the while!
	If Hercules and Lichas play at dice
	Which is the better man, the greater throw
	May turn by fortune from the weaker hand.
	So is Alcides beaten by his rage –

    To win thee, lady. But alas the while!
    If Hercules and Lichas play at dice
    Which is the better man, the greater throw
    May turn by fortune from the weaker hand.
    So is Alcides beaten by his rage –   **35**
    And so may I, blind Fortune leading me,
    Miss that which one unworthier may attain,
    And die with grieving.

PORTIA   You must take your chance,
    And either not attempt to choose at all,
    Or swear before you choose, if you choose wrong,   **40**
    Never to speak to lady afterward
    In way of marriage. Therefore be advised.

MOROCCO   Nor will not. Come, bring me unto my chance.

PORTIA   First, forward to the temple. After dinner
    Your hazard shall be made.

MOROCCO   Good fortune then,   **45**
    To make me blessed or cursèd'st among men!

    Trumpets sound again.

        Exit MOROCCO, *with* PORTIA, *all the others following.*

In this scene ...

- Lancelot Gobbo decides to leave Shylock's service and become one of Bassanio's servants.
- Bassanio agrees to take Gratiano to Belmont with him.

Shylock's servant, Lancelot Gobbo, is torn between staying with Shylock and running away. Just as he decides to leave Shylock's service, his father approaches.

1	**serve**: allow
2	**fiend**: devil
6	**Take heed**: Be careful
8	**Scorn**: Reject
8–9	**with thy heels**: firmly
9	**pack**: leave
10	**'Via!'**: 'Go!'
12–13	**hanging ... heart**: clinging to my heart for comfort
13	**honest**: honourable
15	**honest**: chaste
15–17	**did something ... taste**: was rather sexually promiscuous
20	**counsel well**: give good advice
22	**God ... mark!**: may God forgive me! (like **saving your reverence**, line 24)
25	**incarnation**: He means 'incarnate', i.e. in the flesh / in human form.

THINK ABOUT for GCSE

Performance and staging

- What advice would you offer to an actor performing Lancelot Gobbo's opening speech (lines 1 to 30)?

Themes and issues

- **Hatred and prejudice**: What evidence is there in Lancelot's speech that might suggest that he is prejudiced against Shylock simply because he is a Jew?

Act 2   Scene 2

Venice: a street near Shylock's house.

Enter LANCELOT GOBBO, *alone.*

LANCELOT   Certainly my conscience will serve me to run from
this Jew my master. The fiend is at mine elbow and
tempts me, saying to me 'Gobbo, Lancelot Gobbo –
good Lancelot' – or 'Good Gobbo', or 'Good Lancelot
Gobbo – use your legs, take the start, run away!' My   **5**
conscience says 'No! – Take heed, honest Lancelot,
take heed, honest Gobbo' – or as aforesaid 'honest
Lancelot Gobbo – do *not* run. Scorn running with thy
heels.' Well – the most courageous fiend bids me pack.
'Via!' says the fiend, 'Away!' says the fiend – 'Fore   **10**
the heavens rouse up a brave mind,' says the fiend,
'and run!' Well – my conscience, hanging about the
neck of my heart, says very wisely to me: 'My honest
friend Lancelot, being an honest man's son – or rather
an honest woman's son' – for indeed my father did   **15**
something smack – something grow to – he had a
kind of taste – well, my conscience says 'Lancelot,
budge not!' 'Budge!' says the fiend. 'Budge *not*!' says
my conscience. 'Conscience,' say I, 'you counsel
well. Fiend,' say I, '*you* counsel well.' To be ruled by   **20**
my conscience I should stay with the Jew my master,
who – God bless the mark! – is a kind of devil. And to
run away from the Jew I should be ruled by the fiend,
who – saving your reverence – is the devil himself.
Certainly the Jew *is* the very devil incarnation – and   **25**
in my conscience, my conscience is but a kind of
hard conscience to offer to counsel me to stay with
the Jew. The fiend gives the more friendly counsel.
I will run, fiend – my heels are at your commandment.
I will run!   **30**

Enter OLD GOBBO, *hesitantly, carrying a basket.*

GOBBO   Master young man – you, I pray you, which is the way
to Master Jew's?

Lancelot decides to play a trick on his father, who is almost blind, and persuades him that 'Master Lancelot' is dead.

33–4 true-begotten: true-born
34 sand-blind: half blind
35 try confusions: He may also mean 'try conclusions', i.e. experiment with him; try him out.

40 Marry: Right! (from 'by Saint Mary!')

43 sonties: saints
hit: find
44–5 dwells … dwell with him: usually lives … is at home
46 Master: Lancelot is determined to be called by a gentleman's title.
47 raise the waters: make him cry

51 well to live: still healthy
52 a: he

THINK ABOUT for GCSE

Characterisation

- In what ways is Lancelot different from the characters in the play so far? Think, for example, about his social class, his manner of speech and the things he thinks about.

Language

- Lancelot says his father is 'more than sand-blind' (line 34). The 'sand' comes from 'sam' or 'semi' (half). 'Stone-blind' means totally blind. What do you think Lancelot's invented term 'high gravel-blind' (line 35) means?

55 *ergo*: therefore (Latin)
beseech: beg
57 an't: if it
59 father: term of respect to old men
59–60 Fates … Three: These are all terms for the Fates who, in classical myth, determined a person's life-span.

64 staff: means of support
65 cudgel: thick club
hovel-post: support for a hut

LANCELOT	(*Aside, to the audience*) O heavens! This is my true-begotten father – who, being more than sand-blind, high gravel-blind, knows me not. I will try confusions with him.	35
GOBBO	Master young gentleman, I pray you, which is the way to Master Jew's?	
LANCELOT	(*Turning the old man to face in different directions*) Turn up on your right hand at the next turning, but at the next turning of all on your left. Marry, at the very next turning turn of no hand, but turn down indirectly to the Jew's house.	40
GOBBO	By God's sonties, 'twill be a hard way to hit. Can you tell me whether one Lancelot, that dwells with him, dwell with him or no?	45
LANCELOT	Talk you of young *Master* Lancelot? (*Aside*) Mark me now, now will I raise the waters. – (*To* GOBBO) Talk you of young *Master* Lancelot?	
GOBBO	No 'master', sir, but a poor man's son. His father, though I say 't, is an honest, exceeding poor man, and, God be thanked, well to live.	50
LANCELOT	Well, let his father be what a will, we talk of young *Master* Lancelot.	
GOBBO	Your worship's friend and Lancelot, sir.	
LANCELOT	But I pray you, *ergo*, old man, *ergo* I beseech you, talk you of young *Master* Lancelot?	55
GOBBO	Of Lancelot, an't please your mastership.	
LANCELOT	*Ergo Master* Lancelot. Talk not of Master Lancelot, father – for the young gentleman, according to Fates and destinies, and such odd sayings, the Sisters Three, and such branches of learning, is indeed deceased – or, as you would say in plain terms, gone to heaven.	60
GOBBO	Marry, God forbid! – (*Beginning to weep*) The boy was the very staff of my age, my very prop!	
LANCELOT	(*Aside*) Do I *look* like a cudgel or a hovel-post, a staff or a prop? – (*To* GOBBO) Do you know me, father?	65

49

Having been convinced that his son is dead, Old Gobbo is finally made to believe that he is indeed talking to Lancelot.

67 **Alack the day**: Sad to say / It's very sad

73–4 **a wise … child**: Lancelot gets the proverb the wrong way around. It should be, 'It is a wise child that knows its own father.'

THINK ABOUT for GCSE

Language

• What is distinctive about Lancelot Gobbo's use of language? Look, for example, at his use of classical reference (lines 59 to 61), muddled proverbs (lines 73 to 74) and confused logic (lines 81 to 82).

Performance and staging

• Lancelot Gobbo's treatment of his blind father may seem very cruel to a modern audience. How would you direct it to bring out the comedy and reduce the cruelty? In particular, what opportunities are there for visual or physical comedy?

85 **man**: servant

91 **fill-horse**: cart horse
93–4 **grows backward**: gets shorter rather than longer

96 **agree**: get on

GOBBO	Alack the day! I know you not, young gentleman. But I pray you tell me, is my boy – God rest his soul! – alive or dead?
LANCELOT	Do you not know me, father?
GOBBO	Alack, sir, I am sand-blind. I know you not.
LANCELOT	Nay indeed, if you had your eyes you might fail of the knowing me. It is a wise father that knows his own child. Well, old man, I will tell you news of your son. Give me your blessing.

*He kneels (**but with his back to** OLD GOBBO).*

> – Truth will come to light, murder cannot be hid long – a man's son may, but in the end truth will out.

GOBBO	(*Feeling for* LANCELOT) Pray you, sir – stand up. I am sure you are not Lancelot my boy.
LANCELOT	Pray you, let's have no more fooling about it, but give me your blessing. I am Lancelot – your boy that was, your son that is, your child that shall be.
GOBBO	I cannot think you are my son.
LANCELOT	I know not what I shall think of that – but I *am* Lancelot, the Jew's man, and I am sure Margery your wife is my mother.
GOBBO	Her name is Margery indeed! I'll be sworn, if thou be Lancelot, thou art mine own flesh and blood.

He reaches out to bless LANCELOT, and feels the hair on the back of his head.

> – Lord worshipped might He be! – What a beard hast thou got! Thou hast got more hair on thy chin than Dobbin my fill-horse has on his tail.

LANCELOT	(*Rising*) It should seem, then, that Dobbin's tail grows backward. I am sure he had more hair of his tail than I have of my face when I last saw him.
GOBBO	Lord, how art thou changed! How dost thou and thy master agree? I have brought him a present. How 'gree you now?

70

75

80

85

90

95

Lancelot is telling his father
that he plans to leave Shylock's
service and become Bassanio's
servant instead, when Bassanio
enters.

98–9 set up my rest: staked / gambled all

100 very: real
101 halter: hangman's noose
102 tell: count

105 rare: splendid
     liveries: uniforms

108 I am a Jew if: (like 'I'll be damned if…')
109 hasted: hurried up
110 farthest: latest
111 put … making: arrange for the uniforms
     to be made
112 anon: immediately

THINK ABOUT for GCSE

Themes and issues

- **Hatred and prejudice**:
  What do lines 100 and 108
  suggest about attitudes to
  Jews in Shakespeare's time
  and the ways in which such
  attitudes were reflected in
  common speech?

Structure and form

- In what ways does
  Bassanio's speech to his
  servant help to create a
  sense of bustle and activity
  (lines 109 to 112)?

115 Gramercy: Thank you
     wouldst thou aught: do you want
     anything
117 would: wishes

119 infection: He means 'affection', i.e.
     desire.

123 scarce cater-cousins: not exactly the
     best of friends
126 frutify: He possibly means 'fructify',
     i.e. bear fruit (he is about to give him a
     present), or something like 'certify'.

LANCELOT	Well, well – but for mine own part, as I have set up my rest to run away, so I will not rest till I have run some ground. My master's a very Jew! Give *him* a present? Give him a halter! I am famished in his service – (*Spreading his fingers over his stomach and making his father feel them*) – you may tell every finger I have with my ribs. Father, I am glad you are come. Give me your present to one Master Bassanio, who indeed gives rare new liveries. If I serve not him, I will run as far as God has any ground.

100

105

Enter BASSANIO, *with* LEONARDO *and three other Servants.*

	– O rare fortune – here comes the man! To him, father! – for I am a Jew if I serve the Jew any longer.
BASSANIO	(*To a Servant*) You may do so – but let it be so hasted that supper be ready at the farthest by five of the clock. See these letters delivered, put the liveries to making, and desire Gratiano to come anon to my lodging.

110

Exit the Servant.

LANCELOT	To him, father!
GOBBO	(*To* BASSANIO) God bless your worship!
BASSANIO	Gramercy – wouldst thou aught with me?
GOBBO	Here's my son, sir, a poor boy –
LANCELOT	Not a poor boy, sir, but the rich Jew's man that would, sir – as my father shall specify –
GOBBO	He hath a great infection, sir, as one would say, to serve –
LANCELOT	Indeed, the short and the long is, I serve the Jew, and have a desire – as my father shall specify –
GOBBO	His master and he – saving your worship's reverence – are scarce cater-cousins –
LANCELOT	To be brief, the very truth is that the Jew having done me wrong doth cause me – as my father – being, I hope, an old man – shall frutify unto you –

115

120

125

After some confusing explanations, Bassanio agrees to employ Lancelot, having already discussed the matter with Shylock.

127 **doves**: cooked pigeons

129 **impertinent**: He means 'pertinent', i.e. to do with.

135 **defect**: He means 'effect', i.e. the heart of the matter.
136 **obtained thy suit**: got what you wanted
138 **preferred**: recommended
preferment: promotion

141 **old proverb**: a saying that 'It is enough to have God's grace'
parted: divided
145–6 **inquire ... out**: find out where my house is
146 **livery**: uniform
147 **guarded**: ornamented with trimmings
148 **I cannot ... no?**: Who said I couldn't get a job!
150 **table**: palm of the hand
151 **book**: Bible
152 **Go to**: Look! (i.e. an expression of emphasis)
152–3 **a small trifle of**: just a few
154 **simple**: humble
coming-in: 1 income; 2 sex life
155 **thrice**: three times
156 **with ... feather-bed**: i.e. from some sexual escapade or the danger of marrying
157 **'scapes**: escapes / adventures
158 **gear**: matter / all this

THINK ABOUT for GCSE

Language

• The language used by Lancelot and his father contains malapropisms (mistakenly using a wrong word which sounds similar to the correct one). For each of the following, work out (a) what the correct word should have been, (b) what its intended meaning was, and (c) what the actual, mistaken, meaning was: infection (line 119), frutify (line 126), impertinent (line 129), defect (line 135).

Characterisation

• What does Lancelot Gobbo's 'palm-reading' speech (lines 150 to 159) suggest about the kind of person he is, his ambitions and desires?

GOBBO	(*Offering his basket*) I have here a dish of doves that I would bestow upon your worship, and my suit is –
LANCELOT	In very brief, the suit is impertinent to myself – as your worship shall know by this honest old man – and **130** though I say it, though old man, yet poor man, my father.
BASSANIO	One speak for both. – What would you?
LANCELOT	Serve you, sir.
GOBBO	That is the very defect of the matter, sir. **135**
BASSANIO	I know thee well – thou hast obtained thy suit. Shylock thy master spoke with me this day, And hath preferred thee – if it *be* preferment To leave a rich Jew's service to become The follower of so poor a gentleman. **140**
LANCELOT	The old proverb is very well parted between my master Shylock and you, sir: you have 'The grace of God', sir – and *he* hath 'enough'.
BASSANIO	Thou speak'st it well. (*To* OLD GOBBO) Go, father, with thy son – (*To* LANCELOT) Take leave of thy old master, and inquire **145** My lodging out. (*To another Servant*) Give him a livery More guarded than his fellows' – see it done.
LANCELOT	Father, in. I cannot get a service – no? I have ne'er a tongue in my head – ?

He examines the palm of his hand.

– Well, if any man in Italy have a fairer table which **150** doth offer to swear upon a book – I shall have good fortune! Go to – here's a simple line of life, here's a small trifle of wives – alas, fifteen wives is nothing! Eleven widows and nine maids is a simple coming-in for one man – and then to 'scape drowning thrice, and **155** to be in peril of my life with the edge of a feather-bed – here are simple 'scapes! Well, if Fortune be a woman, she's a good wench for this gear. Father, come – I'll take my leave of the Jew in the twinkling.

Exit, with OLD GOBBO *and another Servant.*

Lancelot celebrates his good fortune. Gratiano comes to ask Bassanio if he can accompany him to Belmont. Bassanio agrees, but on condition that Gratiano calms down and behaves sensibly.

161 orderly bestowed: neatly stowed on board ship

162 feast: hold a feast for

163 best-esteemed acquaintance: closest friends

Hie thee: Hurry / Make haste

164 herein: in this matter

165 Yonder: Over there

THINK ABOUT for GCSE

Performance and staging

- How might the sequence from the Gobbos' departure to Gratiano's meeting with Bassanio (line 159 stage direction to line 169) have been staged in Shakespeare's playhouse? Think about the 'blocking' (stage movements), and particularly the entrances and exits.

Language

- In Shakespeare's time people often used 'thou' when speaking familiarly to a close friend or when speaking to inferiors. What significance is there in Bassanio's switch from 'you' to 'thou' at the beginning of his reply to Gratiano (lines 170 to 171)?

168 suit to you: favour to ask you

169 deny: refuse

171 rude: coarse / uncouth

bold of voice: outspoken

172 Parts: qualities

become thee: suit you

happily: well

174–5 show ... liberal: appear rather too free and easy

175 take pain: make an effort

176 allay: water down

modesty: restraint / moderation

177 skipping: frivolous and thoughtless

178 misconstered: misinterpreted

180 sober habit: 1 serious behaviour; 2 sober / dark clothes

181 but: only

182 demurely: modestly / shyly

183 saying: being said

185 Use ... civility: show all the expected good manners

186 well ... ostent: who has practised looking serious

187 grandam: grandmother

BASSANIO	I pray thee, good Leonardo, think on this: 160
	These things being bought and orderly bestowed,
	Return in haste, for I do feast tonight
	My best-esteemed acquaintance. Hie thee, go!
LEONARDO	My best endeavours shall be done herein.

Enter GRATIANO, *as* LEONARDO *is leaving.*

GRATIANO	Where's your master?
LEONARDO	Yonder, sir, he walks. 165

Exit.

GRATIANO	Signior Bassanio!
BASSANIO	Gratiano!
GRATIANO	I have a suit to you.
BASSANIO	You have obtained it.
GRATIANO	You must not deny me – I must go with you to
	Belmont.
BASSANIO	Why then you must – but hear thee, Gratiano: 170
	Thou art too wild, too rude, and bold of voice –
	Parts that become thee happily enough,
	And in such eyes as ours appear not faults.
	But where thou art not known, why, there they show
	Something too liberal. Pray thee, take pain 175
	To allay with some cold drops of modesty
	Thy skipping spirit – lest through thy wild behaviour
	I be misconstered in the place I go to,
	And lose my hopes.
GRATIANO	Signior Bassanio, hear me:
	If I do not put on a sober habit, 180
	Talk with respect, and swear but now and then,
	Wear prayer-books in my pocket, look demurely,
	Nay more, while grace is saying, hood mine eyes
	Thus with my hat, and sigh and say 'amen',
	Use all the observance of civility 185
	Like one well studied in a sad ostent
	To please his grandam, never trust me more.

Gratiano promises to be on his best behaviour.

188 **your bearing**: how you behave

189 **I bar**: I'm excluding
    gauge: judge / measure
190 **were**: would be a
191 **entreat**: beg

193 **purpose merriment**: intend to have a good time / fun

THINK ABOUT for GCSE

Themes and issues

• What kind of person is Gratiano referring to in his response to Bassanio (lines 180 to 187)? In what ways do his comments contribute to the treatment of **truth and deception** in the play?

Characterisation

• From his appearances in the play so far, what is your impression of Gratiano?

BASSANIO Well – we shall see your bearing.

GRATIANO Nay, but I bar tonight – you shall not gauge me
By what we do tonight.

BASSANIO   No, that were pity.   190
I would entreat you rather to put on
Your boldest suit of mirth, for we have friends
That purpose merriment. But fare you well –
I have some business.

GRATIANO And I must to Lorenzo and the rest –   195
But we will visit you at supper-time.

Exit.
BASSANIO *and Servant go another way.*

In this scene ...

- Lancelot and Jessica, Shylock's daughter, say their farewells.
- Jessica gives Lancelot a letter for Lorenzo and tells the audience of her plans to elope with Lorenzo and become a Christian.

3 Didst rob it ... tediousness: took away some of the boredom

10 exhibit: He probably means 'inhibit', i.e. restrain.
pagan: non-Christian

11 play the knave: 1 have an affair (with your mother); 2 come like a thief

12 get: 1 father / beget; 2 get hold of you (referring to Lorenzo)

12–13 foolish drops: tears

13 something: somewhat

15 Alack: Alas (expression of regret)
heinous: hateful

18 manners: behaviour

19 strife: conflict

THINK ABOUT for GCSE

Characterisation

- Jessica does not tell us why she thinks of her house as 'hell' (line 2). What do we learn in this short scene about her attitudes to living with Shylock?

Relationships

- What does Lancelot Gobbo reveal about his attitude to Jessica in his speech (lines 10 to 13)?

Venice: outside Shylock's house.

Enter Shylock's daughter Jessica, *with* Lancelot.

Jessica	I am sorry thou wilt leave my father so.
	Our house is hell, and thou, a merry devil,
	Didst rob it of some taste of tediousness.
	But fare thee well – (*Giving him money*) there is a
	ducat for thee.
	And Lancelot, soon at supper shalt thou see 5
	Lorenzo, who is thy new master's guest:
	Give him this letter – do it secretly.
	And so farewell – I would not have my father
	See me in talk with thee.
Lancelot	Adieu! Tears exhibit my tongue – most beautiful pagan, 10
	most sweet Jew! If a Christian do not play the knave and
	get thee, I am much deceived. But adieu! These foolish
	drops do something drown my manly spirit – adieu!

Exit.

Jessica	Farewell, good Lancelot.
	Alack – what heinous sin is it in me 15
	To be ashamed to be my father's child!
	But though I am a daughter to his blood
	I am not to his manners. O Lorenzo –
	If thou keep promise I shall end this strife,
	Become a Christian, and thy loving wife! 20

Exit.

In this scene ...

• Lorenzo receives Jessica's letter telling him how she plans to escape from Shylock's house.

As Lorenzo and his friends are making plans for a masque that night, Lancelot arrives with Jessica's letter and tells them that he is off to invite Shylock to dinner with Bassanio.

THINK ABOUT
***for*GCSE**

Context

• A masque was an entertainment or celebration which included music, dancing and the wearing of masks. How might a masque create the ideal opportunity for Jessica to escape from her house with Lorenzo and his friends?

Structure and form

• How successfully has Lancelot Gobbo been used to link the two strands of the plot established so far: Bassanio's attempt to win Portia (the 'caskets plot') and Antonio's dealings with Shylock (the 'flesh-bond plot')?

1   **slink**: sneak / slip

5   **spoke us yet of**: given orders / made arrangements about
    torch-bearers: Masques (see line 23) were often torch-lit.
6   **'Tis vile ... ordered**: It will be worthless if it isn't skillfully planned
9   **furnish us**: prepare

10 **An**: If
    break up this: open this seal
10–11 **seem to signify**: tell you something
12 **hand**: handwriting

15 **By your leave**: If you will excuse me

17 **sup**: have a meal / supper

Venice.

Enter Gratiano, Lorenzo, Salerio *and* Solanio.

Lorenzo	– Nay, we will slink away in supper time,
	Disguise us at my lodging, and return
	All in an hour.
Gratiano	We have not made good preparation.
Salerio	We have not spoke us yet of torch-bearers.

5

Solanio	'Tis vile unless it may be quaintly ordered –
	And better in my mind not undertook.
Lorenzo	'Tis now but four of clock. We have two hours
	To furnish us –

Enter Lancelot, *bringing a letter.*

Friend Lancelot – what's the news?

Lancelot	An it shall please you to break up this, it shall seem to
	signify.

10

Lorenzo	I know the hand. In faith 'tis a fair hand,
	And whiter than the paper it writ on
	Is the fair hand that writ.
Gratiano	Love-news, in faith!
Lancelot	By your leave, sir.

15

Lorenzo	Whither goest thou?
Lancelot	Marry, sir, to bid my old master the Jew to sup tonight
	with my new master the Christian.
Lorenzo	Hold – here, take this (*giving* Lancelot *money*). Tell
	gentle Jessica
	I will not fail her. Speak it privately.

20

Exit Lancelot.

Go, gentlemen –

Lorenzo tells Gratiano what is in Jessica's letter: she plans to take some of her father's money and jewels and escape disguised as Lorenzo's boy torch-bearer in the masque.

22 **masque**: Entertainment with music and dance at which masks were worn.

23 **of**: with

24 **be … straight**: get to work on it straight away

26 **some hour hence**: about an hour from now

29 **directed**: given instructions

31 **furnished**: provided

34 **gentle**: (a play on 'gentile'; see Act 1 Scene 3, line 172)

35 **foot**: path

36–7 **she do … she**: i.e. misfortune personified … Jessica

37 **faithless**: 1 non-Christian; 2 untrustworthy

38 **peruse**: read through

THINK ABOUT for GCSE

Themes and issues

• **Hatred and prejudice**: Now Lorenzo joins other Christian characters in speaking insultingly about Jews. What particular attitudes does he reveal in his final speech (lines 29 to 39)?

Performance and staging

• If you were staging this scene, where would it take place (e.g. in a street, someone's house, an inn), and what importance would the setting have?

	Will you prepare you for this masque tonight?
	I am provided of a torch-bearer.
SALERIO	Ay, marry, I'll be gone about it straight.
SOLANIO	And so will I.
LORENZO	Meet me and Gratiano 25
	At Gratiano's lodging some hour hence.
SALERIO	'Tis good we do so.

Exit, with SOLANIO.

GRATIANO	Was not that letter from fair Jessica?
LORENZO	I must needs tell thee all. She hath directed
	How I shall take her from her father's house, 30
	What gold and jewels she is furnished with,
	What page's suit she hath in readiness.
	If e'er the Jew her father come to heaven,
	It will be for his gentle daughter's sake –
	And never dare misfortune cross her foot, 35
	Unless she do it under this excuse,
	That she is issue to a faithless Jew.
	Come, go with me – peruse this as thou goest.
	Fair Jessica shall be my torch-bearer.

Exit, with GRATIANO.

ACT 2 SCENE 5

In this scene ...

- Shylock is reluctant to leave the house to dine with Antonio and Bassanio.
- Jessica gets ready to make her escape.

Shylock warns Lancelot Gobbo that it will be very different working for Bassanio. Shylock has been invited to dine with Antonio and Bassanio, but he is uneasy about it and reluctant to leave the house.

2 of: between

3 gormandize: over-eat

5 rend apparel out: wear out clothes

8 was wont to: used to
9 bidding: being asked
11 bid forth: invited out
12 wherefore: why
14 upon: at the expense of
15 prodigal: wasteful / spendthrift
16 Look to: look after
right loath: very reluctant
17 ill … rest: trouble brewing which will upset / worry me
18 tonight: last night
19 beseech: beg
20 reproach: harsh criticism (he means 'approach')
21 So do I his: I expect his reproach too
23 masque: entertainment with music and dance
24–6 my nose… afternoon: Lancelot is poking fun at Shylock's superstitions, with a nonsensical series of unnecessary details.
24 my … a-bleeding: A nose bleed was considered a bad omen.
Black-Monday: Easter Monday

Venice: Shylock's house.

Enter SHYLOCK, *with* LANCELOT.

SHYLOCK	Well, thou shalt see, thy eyes shall be thy judge,
	The difference of old Shylock and Bassanio –
	(*Calling his daughter*) What, Jessica! – (*To* LANCELOT)
	Thou shalt not gormandize
	As thou hast done with me – what, Jessica! –
	And sleep, and snore, and rend apparel out.
	Why, Jessica I say!

5

LANCELOT	(*Calling*)	Why, Jessica!

SHYLOCK	Who bids *thee* call? I do not bid thee call.
LANCELOT	Your worship was wont to tell me I could do nothing without bidding.

Enter JESSICA.

JESSICA	Call you? What is your will?

10

SHYLOCK	I am bid forth to supper, Jessica.
	There are my keys. – But wherefore should I go?
	I am not bid for love. They flatter me.
	But yet I'll go in hate, to feed upon
	The prodigal Christian. Jessica, my girl,
	Look to my house. I am right loath to go –
	There is some ill a-brewing towards my rest,
	For I did dream of money-bags tonight.

15

LANCELOT	I beseech you, sir, go – my young master doth expect your reproach.

20

SHYLOCK	So do I his.
LANCELOT	– And they have conspired together. I will not say you shall see a masque, but if you do, then it was not for nothing that my nose fell a-bleeding on Black-Monday last, at six o'clock i' th' morning, falling out that year on Ash-Wednesday was four year in th' afternoon.

25

When Shylock hears about
the masque, he sternly orders
Jessica to shut all the doors and
keep away from the windows.
Lancelot secretly tells Jessica to
look out for Lorenzo. As Shylock
leaves, still full of misgivings,
Jessica looks forward to her
escape.

29 **wry-necked fife**: flute played with the
    musician's head turned sideways
30 **casements**: windows
32 **varnished**: wearing painted masks

34 **foppery**: foolishness

36 **no … forth**: no wish to eat out

41 **worth a Jewess' eye**: 1 worth looking
    at; 2 worth a great deal (proverbial
    expression)
42 **Hagar's offspring**: the children of Hagar
    (in the Bible, an outcast, as Shylock
    considers gentiles to be)
44 **patch**: clown
45 **profit**: progress
46 **wild-cat**: i.e. nocturnal cat
    Drones: Bees that do no work

52 **'Fast … find'**: lock up securely and
    everything will be safe when you return

53 **thrifty**: careful

54 **crossed**: thwarted

THINK ABOUT for GCSE

Language

• What is interesting in
  Shylock's use of language?
  Look, for example, at
  his description of the
  fife's sound (line 29), his
  description of his windows
  (line 33), his use of animal
  references (lines 45 to 46),
  his fondness for Biblical
  allusions (line 35) and
  proverbs (lines 52 to 53).

Relationships

• How would you describe
  the relationship between
  Shylock and Jessica?

SHYLOCK	What, are there masques? Hear you me, Jessica –
	Lock up my doors, and when you hear the drum,
	And the vile squealing of the wry-necked fife,
	Clamber not you up to the casements then, 30
	Nor thrust your head into the public street
	To gaze on Christian fools with varnished faces;
	But stop my house's ears – I mean my casements –
	Let not the sound of shallow foppery enter
	My sober house. By Jacob's staff I swear 35
	I have no mind of feasting forth tonight –
	But I will go. (*To* LANCELOT) Go you before me, sirrah –
	Say I will come.
LANCELOT	I will go before, sir.
	(*Aside, to* JESSICA) Mistress, look out at window for all
	this –
	There will come a Christian by 40
	Will be worth a Jewess' eye.

Exit.

SHYLOCK	What says that fool of Hagar's offspring? – ha?
JESSICA	His words were 'Farewell, mistress' – nothing else.
SHYLOCK	The patch is kind enough, but a huge feeder,
	Snail-slow in profit, and he sleeps by day 45
	More than the wild-cat. Drones hive not with me,
	Therefore I part with him, and part with him
	To one that I would have him help to waste
	His borrowed purse. Well, Jessica, go in –
	Perhaps I will return immediately – 50
	Do as I bid you: shut doors after you –
	'Fast bind, fast find' –
	A proverb never stale in thrifty mind.

Exit.

JESSICA	Farewell – and if my fortune be not crossed,
	I have a father, you a daughter, lost. 55

Exit.

In this scene ...

• Jessica steals money and jewels from Shylock, and runs off with Lorenzo.

Gratiano and Salerio wait outside Shylock's house where they have arranged to meet Lorenzo. He arrives at last and calls out to Jessica.

THINK ABOUT for GCSE

Language

• What is the point Gratiano is trying to make in lines 8 to 19? How do the references to meals, horses and ships help him?

Performance and staging

• In what tone might Lorenzo say 'Here dwells my father Jew' (line 25)?

1   **penthouse**: projecting roof
2   **make stand**: wait
    His ... past: He is almost late (i.e. he should be here by now)
3   **marvel**: remarkable
    out-dwells his hour: is late
4   **ever ... clock**: are always early
5–6 **O ten ... new-made**: people who have only just fallen in love are much keener to keep their love promises
5   **Venus' pigeons**: the doves that drew the love goddess's chariot
6   **wont**: accustomed
7   **obligèd faith unforfeited**: a pledged promise unbroken / marriage vows unbroken
8   **ever holds**: always holds true
9   **appetite that**: appetite with which
10 **untread again**: retrace
11 **measures**: paces
    unbated fire: undiminished enthusiasm
14 **a younger ... prodigal**: a younger son or prodigal son
15 **scarfèd bark**: ship decked with flags
    puts ... bay: sets off from her home harbour
16 **strumpet**: changeable (as a strumpet, or whore, was reputed to be)
18 **over-weathered ribs**: hull damaged by sea and weather
19 **rent**: torn
20 **hereafter**: later
21 **your ... abode**: I apologise for being late
25 **father**: father-in-law (soon-to-be)

ACT 2   SCENE 6

Venice: outside Shylock's house, after dark.

Enter GRATIANO *and* SALERIO, *dressed for the masque.*

GRATIANO   This is the penthouse under which Lorenzo
             Desired us to make stand.

SALERIO   His hour is almost past.

GRATIANO   And it is marvel he out-dwells his hour,
             For lovers ever run before the clock.

SALERIO   O ten times faster Venus' pigeons fly   5
             To seal love's bonds new-made than they are wont
             To keep obligèd faith unforfeited!

GRATIANO   That ever holds. Who riseth from a feast
             With that keen appetite that he sits down?
             Where is the horse that doth untread again   10
             His tedious measures with the unbated fire
             That he did pace them first? All things that are,
             Are with more spirit chasèd than enjoyed.
             How like a younger or a prodigal
             The scarfèd bark puts from her native bay,   15
             Hugged and embracèd by the strumpet wind!
             How like the prodigal doth she return
             With over-weathered ribs and ragged sails,
             Lean, rent, and beggared by the strumpet wind!

Enter LORENZO.

SALERIO   Here comes Lorenzo – more of this hereafter.   20

LORENZO   Sweet friends, your patience for my long abode:
             Not I but my affairs have made you wait.
             When you shall please to play the thieves for wives,
             I'll watch as long for you then. Approach –
             Here dwells my father Jew. (*Calling*) Ho! Who's within? 25

JESSICA, *now dressed as a boy, appears at the window-balcony*
above.

Jessica throws a casket full of jewels down to Lorenzo. She is embarrassed to be disguised as a boy, but agrees to join Lorenzo after she has taken more of Shylock's gold.

27 **Albeit**: although
tongue: voice

33 **pains**: trouble

35 **exchange**: disguise

37 **pretty**: artful

41 **shames**: shameful appearance
42 **good sooth**: truly
light: 1 illuminated; 2 sexually immoral
43 **office of discovery**: job that involves revealing things
44 **should be obscured**: ought to remain hidden
45 **garnish**: decoration (i.e. disguise)
47 **close**: secretive
doth ... runaway: is passing quickly
48 **stayed**: waited
49 **make fast**: secure / lock
gild myself: provide myself (with gold)
50 **straight**: straight away
51 **by my hood**: I swear
gentle: 1 well-bred girl; 2 gentile
52 **Beshrew**: Curse (mild oath)

55–6 **true ... true**: reliable ... constant, faithful

THINK ABOUT for GCSE

Context

• Jessica disguises herself as a boy. In Shakespeare's time, almost all female roles were played by boys or young men. In what ways does Shakespeare draw attention to the fact that a male is playing the role here?

Themes and issues

• **Hatred and prejudice**: What does Gratiano mean by 'a gentle and no Jew!' (line 51)? What does the expression reveal about Gratiano's attitudes?

JESSICA	Who are you? Tell me, for more certainty –
	Albeit I'll swear that I do know your tongue.
LORENZO	Lorenzo, and thy love.
JESSICA	Lorenzo, certain, and my love indeed –
	For who love I so much? And now who knows 30
	But you Lorenzo whether I am yours?
LORENZO	Heaven and thy thoughts are witness that thou art.
JESSICA	Here – catch this casket (*throwing down a small box*)
	– it is worth the pains.
	I am glad 'tis night – you do not look on me –
	For I am much ashamed of my exchange. 35
	But love is blind, and lovers cannot see
	The pretty follies that themselves commit;
	For if they could, Cupid himself would blush
	To see me thus transformèd to a boy.
LORENZO	Descend, for you must be my torch-bearer. 40
JESSICA	What, must I hold a candle to my shames?
	They in themselves, good sooth, are too too light.
	Why – 'tis an office of discovery, love,
	And I should be obscured.
LORENZO	So are you, sweet,
	Even in the lovely garnish of a boy. 45
	But come at once –
	For the close night doth play the runaway,
	And we are stayed for at Bassanio's feast.
JESSICA	I will make fast the doors, and gild myself
	With some more ducats, and be with you straight. 50

Exit above.

GRATIANO	Now, by my hood, a gentle and no Jew!
LORENZO	Beshrew me but I love her heartily.
	For she is wise, if I can judge of her,
	And fair she is, if that mine eyes be true –
	And true she is, as she hath proved herself. 55
	And therefore like herself, wise, fair, and true,
	Shall she be placèd in my constant soul.

As Lorenzo and Jessica leave together, Antonio arrives in haste and tells Gratiano that there is no time for masquing – the wind has changed and Bassanio's ship is ready to sail.

62 **Fie, fie**: 'For goodness' sake!' (expression of impatience)

63 **stay**: wait

64 **is come about**: has changed direction (so the ship can sail)

67 **on 't**: of it

THINK ABOUT for GCSE

Performance and staging

- From the clues in the dialogue and stage directions, how might this scene have been staged in Shakespeare's theatre?

- Since the nineteenth century, many productions have shown a scene in which Shylock returns to find his house empty and Jessica gone. What are the advantages and disadvantages of adding such a scene?

Relationships

- How would you describe Lorenzo's love for Jessica and her love for him?

JESSICA *enters below.*

> – What, art thou come? On, gentlemen – away!
> Our masquing mates by this time for us stay.

Exit, with JESSICA *and* SALERIO.

As GRATIANO *follows the others, enter* ANTONIO.

ANTONIO	Who's there?	60
GRATIANO	Signior Antonio?	
ANTONIO	Fie, fie, Gratiano! Where are all the rest?	
	'Tis nine o'clock – our friends all stay for you.	
	No masque tonight – the wind is come about.	
	Bassanio presently will go aboard –	65
	I have sent twenty out to seek for you.	
GRATIANO	I am glad on 't. I desire no more delight	
	Than to be under sail, and gone tonight.	

Exit, with ANTONIO.

In this scene ...

• The Prince of Morocco fails to choose the correct casket.

The Prince of Morocco begins his choice of the caskets and reads their inscriptions.

1 **discover**: reveal
2 **several**: different

4 **who**: which
5 **Who**: Whoever
8 **dull**: 1 not shiny; 2 too soft to be made sharp
    blunt: 1 not sharp; 2 roughly outspoken (a pun)
9 **hazard**: risk / gamble

12 **withal**: with it / as well

14 **back**: over (in reverse)

THINK ABOUT *for* **GCSE**

Themes and issues

• **Truth and deception**: What do the caskets contribute to a central theme of this play – that appearances can be deceptive?

Performance and staging

• How could you stage this scene? Portia refers to 'curtains' and 'caskets' (lines 1 to 2). Where might they be placed on stage in relation to one another? What might they look like? Where might Portia, Nerissa and Morocco stand and what movements might they make?

19 **fair advantages**: a good profit
20 **dross**: trash
21 **nor give nor**: neither give nor
    aught: anything
22 **virgin hue**: pure colour (Silver was associated with Diana, goddess of chastity.)
25 **with an even hand**: impartially / fairly
26 **be'st ... estimation**: are judged on your reputation / by your own estimate

Belmont: Portia's house.

Trumpets sound.

Enter Portia *with the* Prince of Morocco, *followed by their Servants and Attendants.*

Portia	(*To her Servants*) Go – draw aside the curtains and discover The several caskets to this noble Prince. (*To* Morocco) Now make your choice.

The three caskets are revealed.

Morocco *approaches and examines them.*

Morocco	This first of gold, who this inscription bears: 'Who chooseth me shall gain what many men desire.' The second silver, which this promise carries: 'Who chooseth me shall get as much as he deserves.' This third, dull lead, with warning all as blunt: 'Who chooseth me must give and hazard all he hath.' – How shall I know if I do choose the right?	5 10
Portia	The one of them contains my picture, Prince. If you choose that, then I am yours withal.	
Morocco	Some god direct my judgement! Let me see – I will survey th' inscriptions back again. What says this leaden casket? 'Who chooseth me must give and hazard all he hath.' Must give – for what? For lead? Hazard for lead! This casket threatens. Men that hazard all Do it in hope of fair advantages. A golden mind stoops not to shows of dross – I'll then nor give nor hazard aught for lead. What says the silver with her virgin hue? 'Who chooseth me shall get as much as he deserves.' As much as he deserves! Pause there, Morocco, And weigh thy value with an even hand. If thou be'st rated by thy estimation, Thou dost deserve enough – and yet enough	15 20 25

Morocco gives his reasons for rejecting the lead and silver caskets. He chooses gold because it is the only metal worthy to contain Portia's picture.

THINK ABOUT
for GCSE

Characterisation

• What does Morocco's thinking about the caskets (lines 13 to 60) reveal about him?

Performance and staging

• What advice would you give to the actor playing Morocco on how to deliver this long speech so that it has variety and holds the audience's interest? For example, consider the ways in which each development in his thought processes and decisions might be reflected in the actor's tone, gesture or action.

29 **be afeard of**: doubt / question
30 **Were**: would be
    disabling: belittling

36 **graved**: engraved
40 **shrine**: sacred place (here, a person)
    mortal breathing: living
41 **Hyrcanian deserts**: They are in Persia, famed for their wildness.
    vasty wilds: immense wildernesses
42 **as throughfares**: like highways
44 **watery kingdom**: sea
    head: waves
45 **bar**: barrier
46 **foreign spirits**: courageous travellers from abroad
47 **As o'er a brook**: as if crossing a stream
49 **like**: likely
51 **rib**: enclose
    cerecloth: waxed funeral shroud (i.e. cloth wrapping a corpse)
    obscure: dark
52 **immured**: enclosed / walled in
53 **undervalued to**: less valuable than
    tried: 1 purified; 2 tested
56 **an angel**: The archangel Michael was stamped on the coin called an angel.
57 **insculped upon**: engraved
60 **thrive**: succeed

61 **form**: picture

63 **carrion Death**: rotting skull

May not extend so far as to the lady.
And yet to be afeard of my deserving
Were but a weak disabling of myself.   30
As much as I deserve – why, that's the lady!
I do in birth deserve her, and in fortunes,
In graces, and in qualities of breeding –
But more than these, in love I do deserve.
What if I strayed no further, but chose here?   35
Let's see once more this saying graved in gold:
'Who chooseth me shall gain what many men desire.'
Why, that's the lady! All the world desires her.
From the four corners of the earth they come
To kiss this shrine, this mortal breathing saint.   40
The Hyrcanian deserts, and the vasty wilds
Of wide Arabia are as throughfares now
For princes to come view fair Portia.
The watery kingdom, whose ambitious head
Spits in the face of heaven, is no bar   45
To stop the foreign spirits, but they come
As o'er a brook to see fair Portia.
One of these three contains her heavenly picture.
Is't like that lead contains her? 'Twere damnation
To think so base a thought – it were too gross   50
To rib her cerecloth in the obscure grave.
Or shall I think in silver she's immured,
Being ten times undervalued to tried gold?
O sinful thought! Never so rich a gem
Was set in worse than gold. They have in England   55
A coin that bears the figure of an angel
Stampèd in gold – but that's insculped upon –
But here an angel in a golden bed
Lies all within. Deliver me the key.
Here do I choose, and thrive I as I may!   60

PORTIA   There – take it, Prince. And if my form lie there,
Then I am yours.

MOROCCO *unlocks the golden casket.*

MOROCCO   O hell! What have we here?
A carrion Death – within whose empty eye
There is a written scroll! I'll read the writing.

Morocco opens the gold casket. Discovering that he has chosen wrongly, he leaves disappointed.

65 **glisters**: glitters

68 **my outside**: i.e. gold, of which the casket is made

71 **limbs**: body
    old: mature
72 **inscrolled**: written on a scroll / written here
73 **suit**: wooing
    is cold: has failed
77 **tedious**: long drawn out

79 **complexion**: skin colour

THINK ABOUT *for* GCSE

Themes and issues

• **Truth and deception**: In what ways do Morocco's choice and the contents of the gold casket add to the theme that appearances can be deceptive?

• **Hatred and prejudice**: Portia's concluding comment on Morocco is 'Let all of his complexion choose me so' (line 79). Look back at Act 2 Scene 1, lines 1 to 22 and the first Think About question on page 42. How does Portia's concluding speech in this scene affect your opinion of her? How far do you feel sympathy for Morocco?

'All that glisters is not gold –   65
Often have you heard that told.
Many a man his life hath sold
But my outside to behold.
Gilded tombs do worms infold.
Had you been as wise as bold,   70
Young in limbs, in judgement old,
Your answer had not been inscrolled.
Fare you well. Your suit is cold.'
Cold indeed – and labour lost:
Then farewell, heat, and welcome, frost!   75
Portia, adieu. I have too grieved a heart
To take a tedious leave. Thus losers part.

Exit, with his followers.

PORTIA   A gentle riddance. (*To her Servants*) Draw the curtains
          – go.
          Let all of his complexion choose me so.

Exit, her Servants following.

Act 2 Scene 8

In this scene ...

- Salerio and Solanio describe what happened after Jessica ran off with Lorenzo, and fear for Antonio if he cannot repay the money he owes Shylock.

Salerio and Solanio discuss the outcry following Jessica's elopement. Discussing Shylock's bitter reaction, they express concern about what will happen to Antonio if his ships do not return on time and he fails to repay Shylock's loan.

THINK ABOUT for GCSE

Language

- Look at the language in Salerio and Solanio's account of Shylock's reactions (lines 4 to 24) to Jessica's elopement. Which words and phrases enable them to get the maximum of mockery into their report?

Themes and issues

- **Hatred and prejudice**: From what you know of Salerio and Solanio, how accurate do you think their account of Shylock's behaviour is likely to be?

4 **raised**: roused up

8 **gondola**: canal taxi boat
9 **amorous**: loving

12 **passion**: passionate outcry
13 **variable**: ever-changing
16 **Christian ducats**: 1 gained in interest from Christians; 2 now in Christian hands
19 **double ducats**: ducats worth twice the value
24 **stones**: gems (They are also mocking Shylock: 'stones' could also mean testicles.)

25 **look**: be sure / take care
   keep his day: meets the deadline (for repayment of the loan)
26 **Marry**: by the Virgin Mary (a mild oath)
   well remembered: that reminds me
27 **reasoned**: spoke
28–9 **the narrow ... English**: the English Channel
29–30 **there miscarried a vessel**: a ship was wrecked
30 **fraught**: laden

82

Venice: a street.

Enter SALERIO *and* SOLANIO.

SALERIO   Why, man, I saw Bassanio under sail!
           With him is Gratiano gone along,
           And in their ship I am sure Lorenzo is not.

SOLANIO   The villain Jew with outcries raised the Duke,
           Who went with him to search Bassanio's ship.   5

SALERIO   He came too late – the ship was under sail.
           But there the Duke was given to understand
           That in a gondola were seen together
           Lorenzo and his amorous Jessica.
           Besides, Antonio certified the Duke   10
           They were not with Bassanio in his ship.

SOLANIO   I never heard a passion so confused,
           So strange, outrageous, and so variable,
           As the dog Jew did utter in the streets:
           'My daughter! O my ducats! O my daughter!   15
           Fled with a Christian! O my Christian ducats!
           Justice! The law! – My ducats, and my daughter!
           A sealèd bag – two sealèd bags of ducats,
           Of double ducats, stol'n from me by my daughter!
           And jewels – two stones, two rich and precious stones, 20
           Stol'n by my daughter! Justice! Find the girl!
           She hath the stones upon her, and the ducats!'

SALERIO   Why, all the boys in Venice follow him,
           Crying his stones, his daughter, and his ducats.

SOLANIO   Let good Antonio look he keep his day   25
           Or he shall pay for this.

SALERIO   Marry, well remembered!
           I reasoned with a Frenchman yesterday
           Who told me, in the narrow seas that part
           The French and English, there miscarried
           A vessel of our country, richly fraught.   30

Salerio and Solanio talk about Antonio's great love for Bassanio. He had been very emotional at Bassanio's departure and they decide to go and comfort him.

37–8 **make ... return**: get back as quickly as he could

39 **Slubber not**: Don't spoil by rushing

40 **stay ... time**: wait until the time is right to complete your business properly

42 **mind of love**: thoughts about love

44 **ostents**: displays

45 **conveniently become**: appropriately suit

46 **even there**: at the same moment
big: swollen

48 **affection wondrous sensible**: wonderfully strong / sensitive emotion

50 **he only ... him**: i.e. Bassanio is all Antonio lives for

52 **quicken**: cheer him up from
his embracèd heaviness: 1 the sorrow he has taken on himself; 2 the sorrow he is indulging in

THINK ABOUT for GCSE

Language

• What do you notice about the language Salerio and Solanio use to describe Antonio (lines 35 to 53)? What image of him do they create and by what methods?

Relationships

• From Act 1 Scene 1, and Salerio and Solanio's account in this scene, what impression have you formed of the relationship between Antonio and Bassanio?

	I thought upon Antonio when he told me,	
	And wished in silence that it were not his.	
SOLANIO	You were best to tell Antonio what you hear.	
	– Yet do not suddenly, for it may grieve him.	

SALERIO   A kinder gentleman treads not the earth.   35
            I saw Bassanio and Antonio part.
            Bassanio told him he would make some speed
            Of his return. He answered, 'Do not so.
            Slubber not business for my sake, Bassanio,
            But stay the very riping of the time –   40
            And for the Jew's bond which he hath of me,
            Let it not enter in your mind of love.
            Be merry – and employ your chiefest thoughts
            To courtship, and such fair ostents of love
            As shall conveniently become you there.'   45
            And even there, his eye being big with tears,
            Turning his face, he put his hand behind him,
            And with affection wondrous sensible
            He wrung Bassanio's hand, and so they parted.

SOLANIO   I think he only loves the world for him.   50
            I pray thee let us go and find him out
            And quicken his embracèd heaviness
            With some delight or other.

SALERIO   Do we so.

Exit, with SOLANIO.

In this scene ...

- The Prince of Aragon fails to choose the correct casket.

Another suitor, the Prince of Aragon, prepares to make his choice of caskets. Giving reasons, he rejects lead and gold.

1   **straight**: immediately
2   **Aragon**: (in northern Spain)
3   **comes ... presently**: will now make his choice

6   **Straight ... solemnized**: we will be married straight away
8   **from hence**: away from here

9   **enjoined**: bound
10   **unfold**: reveal

16   **injunctions**: commands

18   **addressed me**: prepared myself

24–5   **be meant by**: mean
25   **fool multitude**: stupid masses
        show: appearances
26   **fond**: foolish
27   **pries not to**: does not look closely into
        martlet: house-martin (a bird)
29   **in ... casualty** where accidents may strike, and with most force

THINK ABOUT for GCSE

Characterisation

- What is the tone of Portia's opening speech (lines 4 to 8)? What does it suggest about her attitude to the Prince of Aragon?

Language

- What will be ironic about Aragon's dismissive comments about 'the fool multitude' (lines 25 to 30)?

ACT 2 SCENE 9

Belmont: Portia's house.

Enter NERISSA, *with a Servant.*

NERISSA   Quick, quick, I pray thee – draw the curtain straight!
           The Prince of Aragon hath ta'en his oath,
           And comes to his election presently.

Trumpets sound, and the three caskets are revealed.

Enter the PRINCE OF ARAGON (*attended by his Servants*)*, and* PORTIA.

PORTIA   Behold, there stand the caskets, noble Prince.
           If you choose that wherein I am contained   5
           Straight shall our nuptial rites be solemnized.
           But if you fail, without more speech, my lord,
           You must be gone from hence immediately.

ARAGON   I am enjoined by oath to observe three things:
           First, never to unfold to anyone   10
           Which casket 'twas I chose; next, if I fail
           Of the right casket, never in my life
           To woo a maid in way of marriage;
           Lastly, if I do fail in fortune of my choice,
           Immediately to leave you, and be gone.   15

PORTIA   To these injunctions everyone doth swear
           That comes to hazard for my worthless self.

ARAGON   And so have I addressed me. – Fortune now
           To my heart's hope! Gold, silver, and base lead.
           'Who chooseth me must give and hazard all he hath.'   20
           You shall look fairer, ere I give or hazard.
           What says the golden chest? Ha – let me see –
           'Who chooseth me shall gain what many men desire.'
           What many men desire – that 'many' may be meant
           By the fool multitude that choose by show,   25
           Not learning more than the fond eye doth teach,
           Which pries not to th' interior, but, like the martlet,
           Builds in the weather on the outward wall,
           Even in the force and road of casualty.
           I will not choose what many men desire,   30

Aragon chooses the silver casket because it promises that the opener will get what he deserves.

THINK ABOUT *for* GCSE

Characterisation

- What do we learn about Aragon's background and character from the thinking that leads up to his choice of caskets (lines 19 to 48)?

Performance and staging

- How might Portia say, 'Too long a pause for that which you find there' (line 52)? Think about how much she knows about the contents of the caskets at this point, the impression she might have formed of Aragon, and the manner in which Aragon may have reacted on opening the casket.

31 **jump … spirits**: ally myself with ordinary people

36–7 **go … cozen**: try to cheat
38 **the stamp of merit**: any deserved entitlement to honours
40 **estates, … offices**: status, rank and official positions
42 **purchased … wearer**: acquired only by deserving people
43 **cover**: keep their hat on (in the presence of an inferior)
bare: with their hat off (in respect to a superior)
45 **gleaned**: weeded out / picked out and rejected
46 **seed**: stock / descendants
47 **chaff**: leavings / trash
48 **new-varnished**: polished up (i.e. reinstated with their true dignities)
50 **assume desert**: lay claim to being worthy
53 **blinking idiot**: (perhaps a winking jester's head)
54 **schedule**: scroll

60 **To … offices**: i.e. It's not for me to say (I cannot comment as I have been the indirect cause of your offence.)
are distinct offices: bring separate responsibilities

62 **tried this**: purified this (i.e. the silver)
64 **amiss**: wrongly

Because I will not jump with common spirits,
And rank me with the barbarous multitudes.
Why, then, to thee, thou silver treasure house:
Tell me once more what title thou dost bear.
'Who chooseth me shall get as much as he deserves.'   35
And well said, too – for who shall go about
To cozen Fortune, and be honourable
Without the stamp of merit? Let none presume
To wear an undeservèd dignity.
O, that estates, degrees, and offices   40
Were not derived corruptly, and that clear honour
Were purchased by the merit of the wearer!
How many then should cover that stand bare!
How many be commanded that command!
How much low peasantry would then be gleaned   45
From the true seed of honour – and how much honour
Picked from the chaff and ruin of the times,
To be new-varnished! Well – but to my choice.
'Who chooseth me shall get as much as he deserves' –
I will assume desert. Give me a key for this,   50
And instantly unlock my fortunes here.

He opens the silver casket.

PORTIA   Too long a pause for that which you find there.

ARAGON   What's here? The portrait of a blinking idiot
Presenting me a schedule! I will read it.
How much unlike art thou to Portia!   55
How much unlike my hopes and my deservings!
'Who chooseth me shall have as much as he deserves'!
– Did I deserve no more than a fool's head?
Is that my prize? Are my deserts no better?

PORTIA   To offend and judge are distinct offices,   60
And of opposèd natures.

ARAGON   What is here?

He reads the message-scroll from the casket.

'The fire seven times tried this –
Seven times tried that judgement is
That did never choose amiss.

Finding the silver casket's contents and reading the scroll, Aragon departs promising to bear his anger patiently. A messenger reports that a young Venetian has arrived to announce the approach of his lord.

65 **shadows**: illusions
66 **a shadow's bliss**: illusory happiness
67 **iwis**: assuredly / certainly
68 **Silvered o'er**: decorated / coated in silver

71 **sped**: done for / finished

73 **By the time**: the longer

77 **wroth**: anger

THINK ABOUT for GCSE

Language

• Shakespeare's verse dialogue is usually in iambic pentameter. What do you notice about the form of the verse in which the scrolls are written (see also Act 2 Scene 7, lines 65 to 73)? What effect is achieved when both Morocco and Aragon deliver a part or all of their exit speech in the same kind of verse (Act 2 Scene 7, lines 74 to 75 and lines 72 to 77 here)?

Characterisation

• What is your final judgement of Aragon? Does his departing speech (lines 72 to 77) allow him a little dignity?

79 **deliberate**: deliberating (i.e. they think too much)
80 **the wisdom ... lose**: enough sense to let reasoning defeat them
81 **heresy**: false belief
82 **goes**: is determined
84 **would my lord**: does my lord want (she mocks his 'my lady')
85 **alighted**: got down from his horse / arrived
86 **A young Venetian**: (possibly Gratiano) **comes before**: has journeyed on ahead
88 **sensible regreets**: material greetings (i.e. gifts)
89 **To wit**: that is to say
commends: words of commendation / praise
courteous breath: polite speeches
90 **Yet**: Until now
93 **costly**: lavish / rich
94 **fore-spurrer**: advance messenger
96 **anon**: next
some kin to thee: one of your relations
97 **high-day**: holiday / 'Sunday best'

	Some there be that shadows kiss –	**65**
	Such have but a shadow's bliss.	
	There be fools alive, iwis,	
	Silvered o'er – and so was this.	
	Take what wife you will to bed,	
	I will ever be your head.	**70**
	So be gone – you are sped.'	
	– Still more fool I shall appear	
	By the time I linger here.	
	With one fool's head I came to woo,	
	But I go away with two.	**75**
	Sweet, adieu. – I'll keep my oath,	
	Patiently to bear my wroth.	

Exit, followed by his Servants.

PORTIA   Thus hath the candle singed the moth.
           O these deliberate fools! When they do choose,
           They have the wisdom by their wit to lose.   **80**

NERISSA   The ancient saying is no heresy:
           'Hanging and wiving goes by destiny.'

PORTIA   Come – draw the curtain, Nerissa.

Enter a MESSENGER.

MESSENGER Where is my lady?

PORTIA   Here. What would my lord?

MESSENGER Madam, there is alighted at your gate   **85**
           A young Venetian, one that comes before
           To signify th' approaching of his lord,
           From whom he bringeth sensible regreets –
           To wit, besides commends and courteous breath,
           Gifts of rich value. Yet I have not seen   **90**
           So likely an ambassador of love.
           A day in April never came so sweet
           To show how costly summer was at hand
           As this fore-spurrer comes before his lord.

PORTIA   No more, I pray thee! I am half afeard   **95**
           Thou wilt say anon he is some kin to thee,
           Thou spend'st such high-day wit in praising him.

Nerissa hopes that the new suitor might be Bassanio.

99 **post**: messenger
   so mannerly: in such an attractive way
100 **Bassanio, ... be!** O Cupid! Please let it be Bassanio!

THINK ABOUT *for* GCSE

Structure and form

• Nerissa has not said a great deal in the two 'casket scenes' (Act 2 Scenes 7 and 9). What functions has she served so far? Look at her contribution to Act 1 Scene 2 and her brief comments here (lines 81 to 82 and 100).

• At the end of Act 2, which questions remain unanswered for the audience? Think, for example, about Shylock's reaction to the loss of Jessica, Antonio's 'bond' with Shylock and the imminent arrival at Belmont of the next suitor.

Come, come, Nerissa – for I long to see
Quick Cupid's post that comes so mannerly.

NERISSA   Bassanio, Lord Love, if thy will it be!   100

Exit PORTIA, *followed by* NERISSA
and the MESSENGER.

Act 3 Scene 1

In this scene ...

- Salerio and Solanio express concern for Antonio after a report that one of his ships has been lost.
- They taunt Shylock, who vows revenge on Antonio.
- Tubal has been unable to find Jessica, but tells Shylock how much she has spent.

As Salerio and Solanio anxiously discuss reports that one of Antonio's ships has been wrecked, Shylock enters and bitterly accuses them of having known about Jessica's elopement.

THINK ABOUT for GCSE

Performance and staging

- How might Shylock enter in this scene? Think about Jessica's elopement and the loss of his jewels.

Language

- How would you describe the language Solanio uses here when talking about Antonio (lines 8 to 14)? What contrasts do you observe when he refers to Shylock (lines 19 to 20)?

2 **yet ... unchecked**: an undisputed rumour is still circulating
3 **lading**: cargo
3–4 **the Goodwins**: dangerous sandbanks in the English Channel
5 **flat**: sandbank
tall: fine / gallant
6 **gossip**: 1 talkative woman; 2 old friend
9 **knapped**: munched / nibbled (proverbially, old women liked ginger)
11 **without ... prolixity**: without slipping into wordiness ('to cut a long story short')
11–12 **crossing ... talk**: preventing clear speech ('beating about the bush')
15 **Come, ... stop**: Finish what you are saying ('Get to the point!')

19 **'amen'**: 'so be it'
betimes: immediately
cross: block / frustrate

25 **wings**: i.e. her disguise
withal: with
27 **fledged**: old enough to fly
complexion: nature
28 **dam**: mother (leading to Shylock's 'damned' wordplay at line 29)

Venice: a street.

Enter Solanio *and* Salerio.

Solanio	Now – what news on the Rialto?
Salerio	Why, yet it lives there unchecked, that Antonio hath a ship of rich lading wrecked on the Narrow Seas – the Goodwins, I think they call the place, a very dangerous flat, and fatal, where the carcases of many a tall ship lie 5 buried, as they say – if my gossip Report be an honest woman of her word.
Solanio	I would she were as lying a gossip in that as ever knapped ginger, or made her neighbours believe she wept for the death of a third husband. But it is true, 10 without any slips of prolixity, or crossing the plain highway of talk, that the good Antonio, the honest Antonio – O that I had a title good enough to keep his name company! –
Salerio	Come, the full stop. 15
Solanio	Ha! What sayest thou? Why the end is, he hath lost a ship.
Salerio	I would it might prove the end of his losses.
Solanio	Let me say 'amen' betimes, lest the devil cross my prayer – for here he comes in the likeness of a Jew. 20

Enter Shylock.

	– How now, Shylock? What news among the merchants?
Shylock	*You* knew, none so well, none so well as you, of my daughter's flight.
Salerio	That's certain. I, for my part, knew the tailor that made the wings she flew withal. 25
Solanio	And Shylock for his own part knew the bird was fledged – and then it is the complexion of them all to leave the dam.

Salerio and Solanio taunt Shylock, who warns them that the bankrupt Antonio must remember the contract he signed. In a passionate speech, he argues that Jews and Christians are not so different.

THINK ABOUT for GCSE

Characterisation

- Reminded that Antonio is now bankrupt, Shylock says 'Let him look to his bond' (lines 40 to 43). Has he always intended to enforce the bond, in your opinion, or does it occur to him only now?

Language

- How does Shylock express his thoughts and feelings in his response to Salerio (lines 46 to 64)? Look at the structure of his argument and his use of grouped clauses, repetition, lists, opposites, and rhetorical questions.

Themes and issues

- **Hatred and prejudice**: How far does Shylock's famous speech about being a Jew lead you to sympathise with him here?

31 **flesh and blood**: child
32 **Out upon it**: Shame on you!
   carrion: rotten meat ('you walking corpse')
   Rebels ... years?: Do you still have uncontrollable sexual urges at your age?
35 **jet and ivory**: black and white
36 **red ... Rhenish**: cheap red and expensive white wines
38 **match**: contract / bargain
   prodigal: man careless with money
40 **smug**: pleased with himself / self-satisfied
   mart: market, the exchange
41 **look to**: remember
   was wont: used
42–3 **for a Christian courtesy**: as an act of Christian generosity
44 **forfeit**: cannot pay you (according to the terms of the bond)
46 **bait fish withal**: use as a bait to catch fish with
48 **hindered me**: prevented me from making / cost me
49 **scorned my nation**: mocked Jews
   thwarted my bargains: messed up / ruined / obstructed my dealings
50 **cooled my friends**: turned my friends away from me
   heated: inflamed
52–3 **dimensions ... affections, passions**: parts of the body ... inclinations, emotions

61–2 **what ... be**: what patient response should he make
63 **execute**: carry out
   it shall go hard: i.e. unless I am prevented
64 **better the instruction**: improve on what I have been taught

SHYLOCK	She is damned for it.	
SALERIO	That's certain, if the devil may be her judge.	**30**
SHYLOCK	My own flesh and blood to rebel!	
SOLANIO	Out upon it, old carrion! Rebels it at these years?	
SHYLOCK	I say my daughter is my flesh and my blood.	
SALERIO	There is more difference between thy flesh and hers than between jet and ivory – more between your bloods than there is between red wine and Rhenish. But tell us, do you hear whether Antonio have had any loss at sea or no?	**35**
SHYLOCK	There I have another bad match – a bankrupt, a prodigal, who dare scarce show his head on the Rialto, a beggar that was used to come so smug upon the mart. Let him look to his bond! He was wont to call me usurer. Let him look to his bond. He was wont to lend money for a Christian courtesy – let him look to his bond!	**40**
SALERIO	Why, I am sure if he forfeit thou wilt not take his flesh. What's that good for?	**45**
SHYLOCK	To bait fish withal! If it will feed nothing else, it will feed my revenge. He hath disgraced me, and hindered me half a million – laughed at my losses, mocked at my gains, scorned my nation, thwarted my bargains, cooled my friends, heated mine enemies – and what's his reason? I am a Jew. Hath not a Jew eyes? Hath not a Jew hands, organs, dimensions, senses, affections, passions? Fed with the same food, hurt with the same weapons, subject to the same diseases, healed by the same means, warmed and cooled by the same winter and summer as a Christian is? If you prick us, do we not bleed? If you tickle us, do we not laugh? If you poison us, do we not die? And if you wrong us, shall we not revenge? If we are like you in the rest, we will resemble you in that. If a Jew wrong a Christian, what is his humility? Revenge. If a Christian wrong a Jew, what should his sufferance be by Christian example? Why, revenge! The villainy you teach me I will execute – and it shall go hard but I will better the instruction.	**50** **55** **60**

As Salerio and Solanio leave
in response to a message from
Antonio, Tubal arrives. He has
searched for Jessica but has been
unable to catch up with her.

67 up and down: everywhere

68 of the tribe: i.e. a Jew
69 matched: found to match them

70 Genoa: port in north-west Italy

74 Frankfurt: (in Germany, famous for its
jewellery fair)
curse: The Christian Bible laid the
blame for Christ's crucifixion on the
Jews, for which they were supposedly
cursed.
77 would: wish
hearsed: placed dead in her coffin

83 satisfaction: compensation
84 lights: settles

89 cast away: wrecked

THINK ABOUT for GCSE

Structure and form

* Actors often call Salerio
and Solanio 'the Salads'.
Why are these characters
in the play? What functions
do they fulfil? Look back at
Act 1 Scene 1, Act 2 Scene
6, Act 2 Scene 8, and this
scene up to and including
the arrival of Tubal.

Characterisation

* How much of Shylock's
passion here is caused by
the loss of his daughter and
how much by the loss of his
jewels, in your opinion?

Enter a SERVANT *of Antonio's.*

SERVANT   (*To* SALERIO *and* SOLANIO) Gentlemen, my master Antonio   **65**
is at his house, and desires to speak with you both.

SALERIO   We have been up and down to seek him.

Enter TUBAL.

SOLANIO   Here comes another of the tribe – a third cannot be
matched, unless the devil himself turn Jew.

Exit, with SALERIO *and the* SERVANT.

SHYLOCK   How now, Tubal! What news from Genoa? Hast thou   **70**
found my daughter?

TUBAL   I often came where I did hear of her, but cannot find her.

SHYLOCK   Why there, there, there, there! A diamond gone cost me
two thousand ducats in Frankfurt! The curse never fell
upon our nation till now – I never felt it till now. Two   **75**
thousand ducats in that, and other precious, precious
jewels! I would my daughter were dead at my foot,
and the jewels in her ear – would she were hearsed
at my foot, and the ducats in her coffin! No news of
them? Why, so! And I know not what's spent in the   **80**
search. Why thou – loss upon loss! The thief gone
with so much, and so much to find the thief – and no
satisfaction, no revenge, nor no ill luck stirring but what
lights on my shoulders – no sighs but of *my* breathing,
no tears but of *my* shedding!   **85**

TUBAL   Yes, other men have ill luck too – Antonio, as I heard
in Genoa –

SHYLOCK   What, what, what? Ill luck, ill luck?

TUBAL   – hath an argosy cast away, coming from Tripolis.

SHYLOCK   I thank God, I thank God! Is it true, is it true?   **90**

TUBAL   I spoke with some of the sailors that escaped the wreck.

SHYLOCK   I thank thee, good Tubal – good news, good news! Ha
ha! – Heard in Genoa!

Shylock is delighted to hear that yet another of Antonio's ships has been lost, but is shocked at the reports of Jessica's spending spree and is especially distraught at the loss of his turquoise ring. He tells Tubal to arrange for an officer to arrest Antonio on the day the bond expires.

95 four score: eighty (i.e. four times twenty)

97 at a sitting: in one go
99 divers: a variety
Antonio's creditors: people to whom Antonio owes money
100 break: become ruined / bankrupt

103 had of: got from
104 for: in exchange for

105 Out upon her!: Damn her! (expression of anger)
106 turquoise: i.e. a precious stone
Leah: probably Shylock's wife
108 undone: ruined
109 fee: hire (to arrest Antonio for debt)
110 bespeak: book
before: i.e. before the day the bond expires
112 make ... will drive whatever bargains I like
113 synagogue: Jewish place of worship

THINK ABOUT for GCSE

Structure and form

- Tubal has only eight short speeches but can make a powerful impact on stage. What dramatic functions does he serve here?

Characterisation

- What are Shylock's motives in having Antonio arrested and forcing him to pay the penalty? Consider, for example, lines 58 to 64, 96 to 100 and 110 to 112, and any other motives apparent from earlier in the play.

- By this point in the play, how sympathetic or otherwise do you feel towards Shylock? Why?

TUBAL	Your daughter spent in Genoa, as I heard, one night, four score ducats.	95

SHYLOCK Thou stick'st a dagger in me – I shall never see my gold again. Four score ducats at a sitting! – Four score ducats!

| TUBAL | There came divers of Antonio's creditors in my company to Venice, that swear he cannot choose but break. | 100 |

SHYLOCK I am very glad of it – I'll plague him, I'll torture him – I am glad of it.

TUBAL One of them showed me a ring that he had of your daughter for a monkey.

| SHYLOCK | Out upon her! Thou torturest me, Tubal – it was my turquoise. I had it of Leah when I was a bachelor. I would not have given it for a wilderness of monkeys. | 105 |

TUBAL But Antonio is certainly undone.

| SHYLOCK | Nay, that's true – that's very true. Go, Tubal, fee me an officer, bespeak him a fortnight before. I will have the heart of him if he forfeit, for were he out of Venice I can make what merchandise I will. Go, Tubal, and meet me at our synagogue. Go, good Tubal – at our synagogue, Tubal. | 110 |

Exit.

TUBAL *goes off in another direction.*

ACT 3 SCENE 2

In this scene ...

- Bassanio chooses the correct casket.
- Gratiano and Nerissa reveal that they want to get married too.
- News comes from Venice that Antonio has lost all his ships and Shylock is demanding justice.

Bassanio has arrived at Belmont. Portia is anxious for him to take time before making his choice, but he is in torment and does not want to wait.

THINK ABOUT for GCSE

Characterisation

- In what ways are Portia's opening words to Bassanio different from those she spoke to Morocco and Aragon? What accounts for that difference? What does she mean by 'though yours, not yours' (line 20)?

Context

- Suspected traitors would be tortured on the rack to make them confess. What does Bassanio mean by 'I live upon the rack' (line 25) and what is Portia implying about his love in her response (lines 26 to 27)?

1 **tarry**: wait
2 **in choosing**: if you choose
3 **forbear**: hold back / wait
5 **would not**: do not want to
6 **Hate ... quality**: hatred does not give that kind of advice
8 **a maiden ... thought**: a modest young woman should not express her feelings openly
10 **venture**: take your chance
11 **then I am forsworn**: I would then be breaking my oath
12 **So ... be**: I will never do that
    So: As a result
14 **Beshrew**: A curse on
15 **o'erlooked**: bewitched
18 **naughty**: wicked
19 **bars**: obstacles
20 **Prove it so**: If it turns out to be so
21 **Let ... not I**: let bad luck be blamed (i.e. I will not have broken my oath)
22 **peize**: slow down
23 **eke it**: eke it out / stretch it / make the best use of it
24 **stay ... election**: delay you making your choice
25 **the rack**: An instrument of torture that stretched the body.
27 **treason**: (crime punished by the **rack**)
28 **mistrust**: anxiety
29 **fear th' enjoying of**: worry that I will never enjoy
30 **amity**: friendship

Act 3 Scene 2

Belmont: Portia's house.

Enter Bassanio *and* Portia (*attended by their Servants*), *with* Gratiano *and* Nerissa.

Portia	I pray you, tarry. Pause a day or two
	Before you hazard – for in choosing wrong
	I lose your company. Therefore forbear a while.
	There's something tells me – but it is not love –
	I would not lose you – and you know yourself,
	Hate counsels not in such a quality.
	But lest you should not understand me well –
	And yet a maiden hath no tongue but thought –
	I would detain you here some month or two
	Before you venture for me. I could teach you
	How to choose right, but then I am forsworn.
	So will I never be. So may you miss me –
	But if you do, you'll make me wish a sin,
	That I had been forsworn. Beshrew your eyes!
	They have o'erlooked me and divided me:
	One half of me is yours, the other half yours –
	Mine own I would say. – But if mine, then yours,
	And so all yours. O, these naughty times
	Puts bars between the owners and their rights!
	And so though yours, not yours. Prove it so,
	Let fortune go to hell for it, not I.
	I speak too long – but 'tis to peize the time,
	To eke it, and to draw it out in length,
	To stay you from election.
Bassanio	Let me choose –
	For as I am, I live upon the rack.
Portia	Upon the rack, Bassanio? Then confess
	What treason there is mingled with your love.
Bassanio	None but that ugly treason of mistrust,
	Which makes me fear th' enjoying of my love.
	There may as well be amity and life
	'Tween snow and fire, as treason and my love.

5

10

15

20

25

30

Portia orders music to be played while Bassanio makes his choice. Comparing him to the hero Hercules, she anxiously stands aside as he approaches the caskets.

THINK ABOUT for GCSE

Language

• As Portia watches Bassanio approach the caskets, she compares him with the hero Hercules (here called Alcides) and herself with Princess Hesione, saved by Hercules from being sacrificed to a sea monster. Nerissa and the others are likened to weeping Trojan (Dardanian) women watching in fear (lines 53 to 62). What meanings do you draw from this extended comparison? Does it convey the idea that Bassanio's choice is a matter of life and death? Or that she is a kind of sacrificial victim being rescued? Or is the comparison of Bassanio with Hercules so ridiculous that it points out another possible truth – that Bassanio, far from being a hero, might be a smooth-talking wastrel, simply after Portia's money?

33 **enforcèd**: compelled (by torture)

38 **for deliverance**: to set me free

42 **aloof**: to one side, at a distance
44 **swan-like**: Swans were believed to sing just before their death.
46 **stand more proper**: be more fitting

49 **Even as the flourish**: just like the trumpet fanfare
51 **dulcet**: sweet

55 **Alcides**: Hercules
56 **howling**: grieving / lamenting
57 **stand for sacrifice**: represent the sacrificial victim
58 **Dardanian wives**: Trojan women
59 **blearèd visages**: tear-stained faces
60 **issue**: outcome
61 **Live thou**: If you live
    dismay: fear
62 **fray**: fight

| PORTIA | Ay, but I fear you speak upon the rack |
| | Where men enforcèd do speak anything. |

| BASSANIO | Promise me life, and I'll confess the truth. |

| PORTIA | Well then, confess and live. |

BASSANIO	'Confess and love'	35
	Had been the very sum of my confession.
	O happy torment, when my torturer
	Doth teach me answers for deliverance!
	But let me to my fortune and the caskets.

PORTIA	Away then! I am locked in one of them.	40
	If you do love me, you will find me out.
	Nerissa and the rest, stand all aloof!
	Let music sound while he doth make his choice –
	Then if he lose he makes a swan-like end,
	Fading in music. That the comparison	45
	May stand more proper, my eye shall be the stream
	And wat'ry death-bed for him. He may win,
	And what is music then? Then music is
	Even as the flourish when true subjects bow
	To a new-crownèd monarch. Such it is	50
	As are those dulcet sounds in break of day
	That creep into the dreaming bridegroom's ear,
	And summon him to marriage.

BASSANIO *approaches the caskets.*

	– Now he goes,
	With no less presence, but with much more love,
	Than young Alcides, when he did redeem	55
	The virgin tribute paid by howling Troy
	To the sea-monster. I stand for sacrifice.
	The rest aloof are the Dardanian wives,
	With blearèd visages come forth to view
	The issue of th' exploit. Go, Hercules!	60
	Live thou, I live. With much, much more dismay
	I view the fight, than thou that mak'st the fray.

Soft music plays.

Still deliberating, Bassanio considers the fact that appearances can often be deceptive.

THINK ABOUT for GCSE

Language

• Neither Morocco nor Aragon made his choice to the accompaniment of music and a song. It has been argued that some of the rhyming words in the song sung here (lines 63 to 71) lead Bassanio to the right casket. How might they do this?

Characterisation

• From what you know of Portia (in particular, look back at lines 10 to 14), how likely is she to help him in this way?

63 **where ... bred**: where does attraction / infatuation originate
65 **begot**: conceived
   nourishèd: fed
67 **is engendered**: originates / is born
68 **With**: by
69 **the cradle**: 1 the eyes; 2 its infancy
70 **knell**: funeral bell
73 **themselves**: what they seem
74 **with ornament**: by appearances
76 **seasoned**: made to sound good
   gracious: charming / eloquent
78 **sober brow**: serious-looking person
79 **approve ... text**: support it by quoting from the Bible
80 **grossness**: flagrant error
81 **assumes**: takes on / acquires
82 **mark ... parts**: outward appearance of good
85 **Mars**: The god of war.
86 **inward searched**: if you look inside them
   have ... milk: are 'lily-livered' (i.e. cowardly)
87 **excrement**: facial hair ('outgrowth')
88 **render them redoubted**: make them look formidable
89 **purchased ... weight**: Cosmetics and false hair were bought by the ounce.
90 **therein**: in that (purchase)
91 **lightest**: 1 least in weight; 2 most frivolous / immoral
92 **crispèd**: tightly curled
93 **wanton gambols**: playful dances
94 **fairness**: beauty
95 **the dowry ... head**: a wig made from a dead woman's hair
96 **sepulchre**: tomb
97 **guilèd**: deceptive / treacherous

BASSANIO *examines the three caskets.*
As he considers and debates his choice, this song is sung.

(SINGER)	Tell me where is fancy bred,
	Or in the heart, or in the head?
	How begot – how nourishèd?

(OTHER VOICES)   Reply, reply.

(SINGER)   It is engendered in the eyes,
                  With gazing fed – and fancy dies
                  In the cradle where it lies.
                  Let us all ring fancy's knell:
                  I'll begin it – Ding, dong, bell.

(OTHER VOICES)   Ding, dong, bell.

BASSANIO   So may the outward shows be least themselves:
                  The world is still deceived with ornament.
                  In law, what plea so tainted and corrupt
                  But, being seasoned with a gracious voice,
                  Obscures the show of evil? In religion,
                  What damnèd error but some sober brow
                  Will bless it, and approve it with a text,
                  Hiding the grossness with fair ornament?
                  There is no vice so simple but assumes
                  Some mark of virtue on his outward parts.
                  How many cowards whose hearts are all as false
                  As stairs of sand, wear yet upon their chins
                  The beards of Hercules and frowning Mars,
                  Who, inward searched, have livers white as milk?
                  – And these assume but valour's excrement
                  To render them redoubted. Look on beauty,
                  And you shall see 'tis purchased by the weight,
                  Which therein works a miracle in nature,
                  Making them lightest that wear most of it.
                  So are those crispèd snaky golden locks
                  Which make such wanton gambols with the wind
                  Upon supposèd fairness, often known
                  To be the dowry of a second head,
                  The skull that bred them in the sepulchre.
                  Thus ornament is but the guilèd shore
                  To a most dangerous sea, the beauteous scarf

65

70

75

80

85

90

95

Rejecting the superficial attractions of gold and silver, Bassanio chooses the lead casket. As he opens it and finds her picture, Portia is ecstatic.

THINK ABOUT for GCSE

Themes and issues

- As he studies the caskets, Bassanio thinks of several instances in which appearances are deceptive. For example, he considers men who pretend to be courageous but are really cowards (lines 83 to 86). What are the other examples he gives in this speech (lines 73 to 107) and what do they contribute to the play's treatment of **truth and deception**?

Performance and staging

- What might Portia do during Bassanio's long speech before choosing a casket? How might she react to it?

99   **Indian**: dark-skinned (Fair skin / hair was considered more beautiful then.)

102   **Midas**: The legendary king whose touch turned everything to gold, including food!

103   **drudge**: servant

104   **'Tween man and man**: Silver was used as money.
  meagre: poor / barren

105   **aught**: anything

106   **eloquence**: fine talking

108   **fleet to air**: vanish into thin air

109   **As**: such as
  rash-embraced: recklessly adopted

111   **allay**: reduce / diminish
  ecstasy: joy

112   **rain**: pour down (with the possible meaning of 'rein', i.e. keep in check)
  scant: limit

114   **surfeit**: have too much / over-indulge

115   **counterfeit**: picture / image
  demi-god: half-god / supernatural creator (i.e. of her image)

117   **the balls of mine**: my eyeballs

118   **severed**: parted / open

119   **bar**: i.e. her breath

120   **sunder**: keep apart
  friends: i.e. her lips

122   **mesh**: net

123   **Faster**: more securely

125   **it**: i.e. the first eye painted
  steal both his: i.e. captivate / dazzle both his eyes

126   **itself unfurnished**: the one painted eye without a partner

127   **substance**: quantity
  shadow: image

128   **underprizing**: 1 undervaluing; 2 failing to praise it adequately

129   **substance**: subject / the real thing (i.e. Portia)

130   **continent**: container

132   **Chance as fair**: gamble as fortunately

Veiling an Indian beauty – in a word,
The seeming truth which cunning times put on   100
To entrap the wisest. Therefore, thou gaudy gold,
Hard food for Midas, I will none of thee –
Nor none of thee (*moving past the silver casket*), thou
   pale and common drudge
'Tween man and man. But thou, thou meagre lead,
Which rather threaten'st than dost promise aught,   105
Thy paleness moves me more than eloquence –
And here choose I. Joy be the consequence!

PORTIA   (*Aside*) How all the other passions fleet to air –
As doubtful thoughts, and rash-embraced despair,
And shuddering fear, and green-eyed jealousy.   110
O love, be moderate, allay thy ecstasy –
In measure rain thy joy, scant this excess!
I feel too much thy blessing. Make it less
For fear I surfeit!

BASSANIO *opens the lead casket.*

BASSANIO   What find I here?
Fair Portia's counterfeit! What demi-god   115
Hath come so near creation? Move these eyes?
– Or whether, riding on the balls of mine,
Seem they in motion? Here are severed lips
Parted with sugar breath – so sweet a bar
Should sunder such sweet friends. Here in her hairs   120
The painter plays the spider, and hath woven
A golden mesh t' entrap the hearts of men
Faster than gnats in cobwebs. But her eyes! –
How could he see to do them? Having made one,
Methinks it should have power to steal both his   125
And leave itself unfurnished. Yet look how far
The substance of my praise doth wrong this shadow
In underprizing it, so far this shadow
Doth limp behind the substance. Here's the scroll,
The continent and summary of my fortune.   130

He reads the scroll from the casket.

'You that choose not by the view
Chance as fair, and choose as true.

Bassanio reads the lead casket's scroll telling him that he can claim Portia as his wife. Portia tells him that she and all her wealth and possessions are now his.

139 **gentle**: kindly / noble
140 **by note**: authorised by the scroll

141 **contending in a prize**: competing in a match

146 **thrice fair**: beautiful three times over
148 **confirmed, signed, ratified**: officially approved (all commercial terms)

THINK ABOUT for GCSE

Language

* Having opened the right casket, Bassanio describes his feelings (lines 141 to 148). What are his feelings, and how effectively does the extended simile describe them?

Themes and issues

* **Money and business**: What commercial language does Bassanio employ in line 148, and Portia in lines 154 to 158? What is its effect here? What might it suggest about their attitudes to their relationship?

150 **for myself alone**: to satisfy my own wishes
151–2 **would ... better**: would not want to be better than I am

155 **That**: so that
account: 1 estimation; 2 reckoning
156 **livings**: possessions
157 **Exceed account**: be too high a figure to calculate
158 **term in gross**: name in total
159 **unpractised**: inexperienced

167 **converted**: changed
But now: Just now
169 **even now, but now**: in this very moment

Since this fortune falls to you,
Be content, and seek no new.
If you be well pleased with this,   135
And hold your fortune for your bliss,
Turn you where your lady is
And claim her with a loving kiss.'
A gentle scroll! Fair lady, by your leave,
I come by note to give, and to receive.   140

He kisses PORTIA.

Like one of two contending in a prize
That thinks he hath done well in people's eyes,
Hearing applause and universal shout,
Giddy in spirit, still gazing in a doubt
Whether those peals of praise be his or no –   145
So, thrice-fair lady, stand I even so,
As doubtful whether what I see be true,
Until confirmed, signed, ratified by you.

PORTIA   You see me, Lord Bassanio, where I stand,
Such as I am. Though for myself alone   150
I would not be ambitious in my wish
To wish myself much better, yet for you
I would be trebled twenty times myself –
A thousand times more fair, ten thousand times more
    rich,
That only to stand high in your account,   155
I might in virtues, beauties, livings, friends,
Exceed account. But the full sum of me
Is sum of something which, to term in gross,
Is an unlessoned girl, unschooled, unpractised –
Happy in this, she is not yet so old   160
But she may learn – happier than this,
She is not bred so dull but she can learn.
Happiest of all, is that her gentle spirit
Commits itself to yours to be directed,
As from her lord, her governor, her king.   165
Myself, and what is mine, to you and yours
Is now converted. But now I was the lord
Of this fair mansion, master of my servants,
Queen o'er myself – and even now, but now,

Portia gives Bassanio a ring, saying that, if he ever loses it or gives it away, it will mean that he has stopped loving her. Bassanio promises to keep the ring until his dying day.

173 presage: foretell / indicate
174 vantage to exclaim on: opportunity to accuse / complain
175 bereft: robbed
176 blood: passion / life
177 powers: faculties / ability to think and speak
178 oration: public speech
181 something: small utterance
blent: blended
182 wild: confused sound
save: except

THINK ABOUT for GCSE

Characterisation

• What does Portia's response to Bassanio's choice of caskets reveal about her view of her own worth (lines 150 to 157); her weaknesses and deficiencies (lines 157 to 159); her willingness to be ruled by Bassanio (lines 159 to 165); her readiness to hand over all her property to him (lines 166 to 171)? What is your opinion of Portia after this speech?

Context

• In history, a woman's property has often been under the control of her father and then, when she married, her husband. How far does that fact help you to understand Portia's words to Bassanio (lines 166 to 174)?

185 be bold to say: you may certainly say

193 bargain: contract
194 Even: exactly
195 so thou canst: provided you can

198 maid: waiting gentlewoman
199– 200 intermission … you: I don't like delaying any more than you do
201 stood: depended
202 the matter falls: it turns out

204 roof: roof of my mouth

	This house, these servants, and this same myself	170
	Are yours – my lord's. I give them with this ring –	
	Which when you part from, lose, or give away,	
	Let it presage the ruin of your love,	
	And be my vantage to exclaim on you.	

BASSANIO   Madam, you have bereft me of all words.   175
Only my blood speaks to you in my veins –
And there is such confusion in my powers,
As after some oration fairly spoke
By a belovèd prince, there doth appear
Among the buzzing pleasèd multitude –   180
Where every something being blent together,
Turns to a wild of nothing, save of joy
Expressed, and not expressed.

He puts on the ring.

            – But when this ring
Parts from this finger, then parts life from hence –
O then be bold to say Bassanio's dead!   185

NERISSA   My lord and lady, it is now our time
That have stood by and seen our wishes prosper,
To cry 'Good joy'. Good joy, my lord and lady!

GRATIANO   My lord Bassanio, and my gentle lady,
I wish you all the joy that you can wish,   190
For I am sure you can wish none from me.
And when your honours mean to solemnize
The bargain of your faith, I do beseech you
Even at that time I may be married too.

BASSANIO   With all my heart, so thou canst get a wife.   195

GRATIANO   I thank your lordship, you have got me one.
My eyes, my lord, can look as swift as yours:
You saw the mistress, I beheld the maid.
You loved, I loved – for intermission
No more pertains to me, my lord, than you.   200
Your fortune stood upon the caskets there,
And so did mine too, as the matter falls.
For wooing here until I sweat again,
And swearing till my very roof was dry

Gratiano and Nerissa reveal that they too want to get married. As the two couples are sharing a joke, Lorenzo, Jessica, and Salerio arrive from Venice.

THINK ABOUT *for* **GCSE**

Performance and staging

• How might Gratiano and Nerissa behave during Bassanio's choice of the caskets (they have no dialogue)? Do they reveal their anxiety – given that Nerissa has agreed to marry Gratiano only if Bassanio wins Portia (lines 206 to 208 – or might any action on their part distract and confuse the audience?

Characterisation

• Gratiano tells Bassanio that he wants to marry. What do Bassanio's responses suggest about his attitude to Gratiano (lines 195 and 210)? How similar is it to the attitude Bassanio conveyed in Act 2 Scene 2, lines 170 to 179?

209 **so ... withal**: if it is acceptable to you

213 **play ... boy**: bet who has the first son

215 **stake down**: putting money down in advance to cover the bet (there is a sexual meaning in 'stake', i.e. penis.)

217 **infidel**: non-Christian

220 **youth**: newness
     new interest: recently acquired authority

222 **very**: true

224 **entirely**: heartily

228 **did entreat**: begged
     past ... nay: so that it was impossible to refuse

231 **Commends him**: sends his regards

	With oaths of love, at last – if promise last –	205
	I got a promise of this fair one here	
	To have her love, provided that your fortune	
	Achieved her mistress.	

PORTIA   Is this true, Nerissa?

NERISSA   Madam, it is, so you stand pleased withal.

BASSANIO   And do you, Gratiano, mean good faith?   210

GRATIANO   Yes – faith, my lord.

BASSANIO   Our feast shall be much honoured in your marriage.

GRATIANO   (*To* NERISSA) We'll play with them the first boy for a
           thousand ducats!

NERISSA   What! – and stake down?   215

GRATIANO   No – we shall ne'er win at that sport and stake down.
           But who comes here? Lorenzo and his infidel!
           What! – and my old Venetian friend Salerio?

Enter LORENZO, JESSICA, *and* SALERIO.

BASSANIO   Lorenzo and Salerio, welcome hither –
           If that the youth of my new interest here   220
           Have power to bid you welcome. By your leave
           I bid my very friends and countrymen,
           Sweet Portia, welcome.

PORTIA   So do I my lord:
           They are entirely welcome.

LORENZO   I thank your honour. For my part, my lord,   225
           My purpose was not to have seen you here,
           But meeting with Salerio by the way,
           He did entreat me, past all saying nay,
           To come with him along.

SALERIO   I did, my lord,
           And I have reason for it. Signior Antonio   230
           Commends him to you.

He gives BASSANIO *a letter.*

Gratiano tells Salerio about their successful wooing and asks for news of Antonio. Bassanio is shocked when he reads Antonio's letter, and he tells Portia what he owes Antonio.

231 **Ere I ope**: Before I open

233 **in mind**: emotionally
234 **in mind**: he has enough strength of mind
235 **estate**: circumstances

236 **cheer yond stranger**: welcome the newcomer over there (i.e. Jessica)

240 **Jasons ... fleece**: Jason and the Argonauts quested for the Golden Fleece.
242 **shrewd**: 1 painful; 2 ominous

245 **turn ... constitution**: disturb the mind and body
246 **constant**: stable and healthy
247 **leave**: your permission

251 **blotted**: spoilt / stained
252 **impart**: declare
254 **Ran in my veins**: was in my blood (as a gentleman)

256 **Rating**: estimating
257 **braggart**: boaster
258 **state**: wealth

260 **have engaged myself to**: am in debt to
261 **mere**: absolute / total
262 **feed my means**: provide me with what I needed

THINK ABOUT for GCSE

Characterisation

• When Jessica arrived, Gratiano referred to her as Lorenzo's 'infidel' (line 217). Here he says, 'Nerissa, cheer yond stranger – bid her welcome' (line 236). What is his attitude to Jessica?

Themes and issues

• **Money and business**: Look back at Act 1 Scene 1, lines 170 to 172 and the second Think About question on page 18. The legend of the Golden Fleece is used in Act 1 Scene 1 in connection with the many suitors who came in quest of Portia. What is the effect of the further reference to it here (lines 239 to 240)?

| BASSANIO | Ere I ope his letter, |
| | I pray you tell me how my good friend doth. |

SALERIO	Not sick, my lord, unless it be in mind,
	Nor well, unless in mind. His letter there
	Will show you his estate. 235

BASSANIO *opens the letter.*

GRATIANO	Nerissa, cheer yond stranger – bid her welcome.
	Your hand, Salerio – what's the news from Venice?
	How doth that royal merchant, good Antonio?
	I know he will be glad of our success:
	We are the Jasons, we have won the fleece. 240

| SALERIO | I would you had won the fleece that he hath lost. |

PORTIA	There are some shrewd contents in yond same paper
	That steals the colour from Bassanio's cheek –
	Some dear friend dead, else nothing in the world
	Could turn so much the constitution 245
	Of any constant man. What, worse and worse?
	With leave, Bassanio, I am half yourself,
	And I must freely have the half of anything
	That this same paper brings you.

BASSANIO	O sweet Portia,
	Here are a few of the unpleasant'st words 250
	That ever blotted paper! Gentle lady,
	When I did first impart my love to you,
	I freely told you all the wealth I had
	Ran in my veins – I was a gentleman –
	And then I told you true. And yet, dear lady, 255
	Rating myself at nothing, you shall see
	How much I was a braggart. When I told you
	My state was nothing, I should then have told you
	That I was worse than nothing – for indeed
	I have engaged myself to a dear friend, 260
	Engaged my friend to his mere enemy,
	To feed my means. Here is a letter, lady –
	The paper as the body of my friend,
	And every word in it a gaping wound
	Issuing life-blood. – But is it true, Salerio? 265

Portia hears about Antonio's bond with Shylock and the loss of Antonio's ships. Salerio reports that Shylock is demanding justice, and Jessica confirms that her father is determined to carry through his revenge on Antonio.

THINK ABOUT
for GCSE

Characterisation

- What might Jessica's emotions be at this point? How does she feel as a visitor to Belmont? In your opinion, is she right or wrong to speak out against her father (lines 283 to 289)?

- How important are Jessica's words in helping us to understand Shylock's real motives in offering the bond?

- What particular contrasts are drawn between Shylock and Antonio, according to the descriptions by Salerio (lines 271 to 282) and Bassanio (lines 291 to 295)?

266 **ventures**: investments
 hit: was successful
268 **Barbary**: the north-west coast of Africa

270 **merchant-marring**: which destroy merchant ships

271 **should appear**: appears
272 **present**: ready
 discharge: pay off
275 **confound**: destroy
276 **plies**: pesters
277 **impeach … state**: makes accusations which harm Venice's reputation for justice
279–80 **magnificoes … port**: most influential noblemen
280 **persuaded with**: argued with / entreated
281 **envious**: malicious
282 **forfeiture**: penalty (i.e. for breaking the contract)

288 **deny not**: do not prevent it
289 **hard with**: very badly for

292 **best-conditioned**: most good-natured
293 **courtesies**: kind, generous acts
294 **ancient Roman honour**: sense of honour that made Romans act out of the highest motives

298 **deface**: tear up / cancel

| | Hath all his ventures failed? What, not one hit?
From Tripolis, from Mexico, and England,
From Lisbon, Barbary, and India,
And not one vessel 'scape the dreadful touch
Of merchant-marring rocks? | |

SALERIO   Not one, my lord.   270
Besides, it should appear that if he had
The present money to discharge the Jew,
He would not take it. Never did I know
A creature that did bear the shape of man
So keen and greedy to confound a man.   275
He plies the Duke at morning and at night,
And doth impeach the freedom of the state
If they deny him justice. Twenty merchants,
The Duke himself, and the magnificoes
Of greatest port have all persuaded with him,   280
But none can drive him from the envious plea
Of forfeiture, of justice, and his bond.

JESSICA   When I was with him I have heard him swear
To Tubal and to Chus, his countrymen,
That he would rather have Antonio's flesh   285
Than twenty times the value of the sum
That he did owe him. And I know, my lord,
If law, authority, and power deny not,
It will go hard with poor Antonio.

PORTIA   Is it your dear friend that is thus in trouble?   290

BASSANIO   The dearest friend to me, the kindest man,
The best-conditioned and unwearied spirit
In doing courtesies – and one in whom
The ancient Roman honour more appears
Than any that draws breath in Italy.   295

PORTIA   What sum owes he the Jew?

BASSANIO   For me, three thousand ducats.

PORTIA   What – no more?
Pay him six thousand, and deface the bond.
Double six thousand, and then treble that,
Before a friend of this description   300

Portia offers to pay Shylock much more than he is owed and tells Bassanio to set off for Venice in order to settle the debt. Bassanio reads out Antonio's letter and promises to return as soon as he can.

310 **hence**: go away
312 **dear ... dear**: expensively (either it has cost Portia a lot to 'buy' him, or Antonio has risked a lot for him) ... deeply
314 **miscarried**: been lost
314–5 **my creditors**: people to whom I owe money
315 **estate**: condition
318–9 **Notwithstanding, ... pleasure**: Despite all that, do as you wish

THINK ABOUT for GCSE

Structure and form

- It is often argued that Shakespeare contrasts the worlds of Venice and Belmont in this play. What differences do you observe? Are there any important similarities between the two settings?

Performance and staging

- How might the two locations of Venice and Belmont be made to look different in a stage production?

321 **dispatch**: settle / complete / hurry

322 **good leave**: willing permission

325 **be ... twain** will come between us two

Shall lose a hair through Bassanio's fault.
First go with me to church, and call me wife,
And then away to Venice to your friend.
For never shall you lie by Portia's side
With an unquiet soul. You shall have gold   305
To pay the petty debt twenty times over.
When it is paid, bring your true friend along.
My maid Nerissa and myself meantime
Will live as maids and widows. Come – away! –
For you shall hence upon your wedding day.   310
Bid your friends welcome, show a merry cheer –
Since you are dear bought, I will love you dear.
But let me hear the letter of your friend.

BASSANIO   (*Reads*) 'Sweet Bassanio – my ships have all miscarried, my
creditors grow cruel, my estate is very low. My bond to   315
the Jew is forfeit – and since, in paying it, it is impossible
I should live, all debts are cleared between you and I, if
I might but see you at my death. Notwithstanding, use
your pleasure: if your love do not persuade you to come,
let not my letter.'   320

PORTIA   O love – dispatch all business and be gone!

BASSANIO   Since I have your good leave to go away,
I will make haste. But till I come again,
No bed shall e'er be guilty of my stay,
Nor rest be interposer 'twixt us twain.   325

Exit, with PORTIA. *The others follow.*

ACT 3   SCENE 3

In this scene ...

• Shylock refuses to consider Antonio's pleas for mercy.

Antonio has persuaded the jailer
to let him come out of prison to
appeal to Shylock for mercy, but
Shylock refuses to listen to his
pleas.

9 **naughty**: useless / wicked
   art so fond: are so stupid / foolish
10 **come abroad**: walk the streets

14 **dull-eyed**: gullible / easily deceived
16 **intercessors**: people who plead on
   behalf of others

18 **impenetrable**: hard-hearted / immovable
   cur: dog
19 **kept**: lived

THINK ABOUT
for **GCSE**

Characterisation

• What does this scene reveal
  about Shylock? How far is
  he motivated by revenge, in
  your opinion?

• What motivates Shylock,
  according to Antonio (lines
  21 to 24)?

20 **bootless**: pointless
22 **oft delivered**: often freed
   forfeitures: penalties
23 **made moan**: complained
24 **Therefore**: That is why

Venice: a street.

Enter Shylock, Antonio (*in the custody of a Jailer*), *and* Solanio.

Shylock	Jailer, look to him. Tell not me of mercy.
	This is the fool that lent out money gratis –
	Jailer, look to him.
Antonio	Hear me yet, good Shylock –
Shylock	I'll have my bond – speak not against my bond!
	I have sworn an oath that I will have my bond. 5
	Thou call'dst me dog before thou hadst a cause,
	But since I am a dog, beware my fangs.
	The Duke shall grant me justice. I do wonder,
	Thou naughty jailer, that thou art so fond
	To come abroad with him at his request. 10
Antonio	I pray thee hear me speak.
Shylock	I'll have my bond! I will not hear thee speak.
	I'll have my bond, and therefore speak no more.
	I'll not be made a soft and dull-eyed fool,
	To shake the head, relent, and sigh, and yield 15
	To Christian intercessors. (*He turns to go.*) Follow not –
	I'll have no speaking! I will have my bond.

Exit.

Solanio	It is the most impenetrable cur
	That ever kept with men.
Antonio	Let him alone.
	I'll follow him no more with bootless prayers. 20
	He seeks my life, his reason well I know:
	I oft delivered from his forfeitures
	Many that have at times made moan to me.
	Therefore he hates me.
Solanio	I am sure the Duke
	Will never grant this forfeiture to hold. 25
Antonio	The Duke cannot deny the course of law –

Antonio knows that the Duke will not be able to bend the law just to get him off the hook.

27 **commodity**: benefits / privileges (commercial term)
   strangers: outsiders (i.e. including Venetian Jews)
29 **much … state** cause the city's reputation for justice to be greatly discredited
31 **Consisteth of**: depends upon the fair treatment of
32 **so bated me**: caused me to lose so much weight

THINK ABOUT for GCSE

Themes and issues

• **Law, justice and mercy**: According to Antonio, why cannot the Duke simply cancel the bond and release Antonio from having to pay the forfeit (lines 26 to 31)?

Structure and form

• What are the main purposes of this short scene?

For the commodity that strangers have
With us in Venice, if it be denied,
Will much impeach the justice of the state,
Since that the trade and profit of the city   30
Consisteth of all nations. Therefore go.
These griefs and losses have so bated me
That I shall hardly spare a pound of flesh
Tomorrow, to my bloody creditor.
Well, jailer – on. Pray God Bassanio come   35
To see me pay his debt, and then I care not.

Exit (escorted by the Jailer), with SOLANIO.

In this scene ...

• Portia appoints Lorenzo master of the house in her absence and begins to reveal her plans to Nerissa.

Lorenzo praises Portia, especially for encouraging Bassanio to go to Antonio's aid. Portia temporarily hands over control of her house to Lorenzo and Jessica, explaining that she and Nerissa are planning to stay in a nearby monastery until their husbands return.

2 **conceit**: understanding
3 **god-like amity**: divine friendship

7 **lover**: friend
9 **customary ... you**: ordinary generosity would make you

10 **repent for**: regret

12 **waste**: pass / while away
13 **bear ... love**: love each other equally
14 **needs**: of necessity / necessarily
   like proportion: similar balance
15 **lineaments**: characteristics / physical features
17 **bosom lover**: intimate friend
19 **bestowed**: given / paid
20 **semblance**: image

25 **husbandry and manage**: domestic care and management

28 **contemplation**: meditation

32 **abide**: stay
33 **deny this imposition**: refuse this task imposed upon you

THINK ABOUT for GCSE

Themes and issues

• **Love and friendship**: The play so far has featured a number of loving relationships. They include the relationships between Portia and Bassanio, Antonio and Bassanio, and Lorenzo and Jessica. What is the nature of the 'love' that each of these six characters experiences? How would you describe each experience?

ACT 3   SCENE 4

Belmont: Portia's house.

Enter PORTIA, *with* NERISSA, LORENZO, JESSICA *and* BALTHAZAR
(*a servant of Portia's*).

LORENZO	Madam, although I speak it in your presence,
	You have a noble and a true conceit
	Of god-like amity, which appears most strongly
	In bearing thus the absence of your lord.
	But if you knew to whom you show this honour,

5

How true a gentleman you send relief,
How dear a lover of my lord your husband,
I know you would be prouder of the work
Than customary bounty can enforce you.

PORTIA   I never did repent for doing good,   10
Nor shall not now. For in companions
That do converse and waste the time together,
Whose souls do bear an equal yoke of love,
There must be needs a like proportion
Of lineaments, of manners, and of spirit –   15
Which makes me think that this Antonio,
Being the bosom lover of my lord,
Must needs be like my lord. If it be so,
How little is the cost I have bestowed
In purchasing the semblance of my soul   20
From out the state of hellish cruelty!
This comes too near the praising of myself,
Therefore no more of it: hear other things.
Lorenzo, I commit into your hands
The husbandry and manage of my house   25
Until my lord's return. For mine own part,
I have toward heaven breathed a secret vow
To live in prayer and contemplation,
Only attended by Nerissa here,
Until her husband and my lord's return.   30
There is a monastery two miles off,
And there we will abide. I do desire you
Not to deny this imposition,

Portia sends her servant
Balthazar to Padua to collect
certain papers and clothes from
her cousin, Doctor Bellario, and
begins to unfold her plans to
Nerissa.

34 The which: which

37 people: servants / household
38 acknowledge: regard (as master and
mistress)

46 honest-true: truthful and reliable
49 Padua: An Italian city famous for its
university and law school.
render: give

51 look what: whatever
52 imagined: all imaginable
53 traject: ferry
common: public
54 trades: crosses / communicates with
56 convenient: appropriate

60 a habit: clothes
61 accomplishèd: equipped
62 that we lack: what we lack (i.e. male
sex organs)
hold ... wager: offer you any bet
63 accoutred: kitted out / clothed

The which my love and some necessity
Now lays upon you.

LORENZO   Madam, with all my heart   35
I shall obey you in all fair commands.

PORTIA My people do already know my mind,
And will acknowledge you and Jessica
In place of Lord Bassanio and myself.
So fare you well till we shall meet again.   40

LORENZO Fair thoughts and happy hours attend on you!

JESSICA I wish your ladyship all heart's content.

PORTIA I thank you for your wish, and am well pleased
To wish it back on you: fare you well, Jessica.

Exit JESSICA, *with* LORENZO.

– Now, Balthazar,   45
As I have ever found thee honest-true,
So let me find thee still. Take this same letter,
And use thou all th' endeavour of a man
In speed to Padua. See thou render this
Into my cousin's hand, Doctor Bellario,   50
And look what notes and garments he doth give thee.
Bring them, I pray thee, with imagined speed
Unto the traject, to the common ferry
Which trades to Venice. Waste no time in words,
But get thee gone. I shall be there before thee.   55

BALTHAZAR Madam, I go with all convenient speed.

Exit.

PORTIA Come on, Nerissa, I have work in hand
That you yet know not of. We'll see our husbands
Before they think of us.

NERISSA   Shall *they* see us?

PORTIA They shall, Nerissa, but in such a habit   60
That they shall think we are accomplishèd
With that we lack. I'll hold thee any wager,
When we are both accoutred like young men,

Portia plans to disguise herself and Nerissa as young men and journey to Venice.

65 **the braver grace**: more style
66 **between ... boy**: as though my voice were breaking
67 **reed**: reedy / high
    mincing: dainty
68 **frays**: fights
69 **quaint**: clever / ingenious
71 **Which I denying**: and when I rejected them
72 **do withal**: help it
74 **puny**: pathetic (told by inexperienced boys)
75–6 **discontinued ... twelvemonth**: left school just over a year ago
77 **raw**: immature
    jacks: fellows / lads
78 **turn to**: be transformed into
79 **Fie!**: Shame on you!
80 **a lewd interpreter**: someone who saw a dirty meaning ('turn to men' can mean 'invite men to have sex with us'.)
81 **device**: plan
82 **stays**: waits
84 **measure**: cover

THINK ABOUT for GCSE

Context

• From Portia's mocking speech (lines 62 to 78), how might we assume some immature young men typically behaved in Shakespeare's time?

• Portia and Nerissa would have been played by boys or young men in Shakespeare's playhouse. In what ways might the effect have been different when a young male actor spoke lines 62 to 78 to an Elizabethan audience?

I'll prove the prettier fellow of the two,
And wear my dagger with the braver grace,   65
And speak between the change of man and boy
With a reed voice, and turn two mincing steps
Into a manly stride, and speak of frays
Like a fine bragging youth – and tell quaint lies
How honourable ladies sought my love –   70
Which I denying, they fell sick and died –
I could not do withal. Then I'll repent,
And wish, for all that, that I had not killed them.
And twenty of these puny lies I'll tell,
That men shall swear I've discontinued school   75
Above a twelvemonth. I have within my mind
A thousand raw tricks of these bragging jacks
Which I will practise.

NERISSA   Why – shall we turn to men?

PORTIA   Fie! – What a question's that,
If thou wert near a lewd interpreter!   80
But come, I'll tell thee all my whole device
When I am in my coach, which stays for us
At the park gate – and therefore haste away,
For we must measure twenty miles today.

                              Exit, followed by NERISSA.

131

In this scene ...

- Lancelot Gobbo and Jessica discuss her having become a Christian.
- Lorenzo and Jessica talk about Portia's excellent qualities.

Lancelot fears that Jessica might be damned for being Shylock's daughter. She reminds him that, in marrying Lorenzo, she has become a Christian.

THINK ABOUT for GCSE

Context

- In Shakespeare's time there was sometimes concern among Christians about the fact that some Jews were converting to Christianity. How is that concern reflected in this scene?

Performance and staging

- What movements and actions might accompany Lancelot and Jessica's dialogue up to Lorenzo's opening speech (line 26)?

1–2 **the sins ... children**: children are to be punished for their father's sins (from the Bible)

2 **promise**: assure

3 **fear you**: fear for you
plain: frank

4 **agitation**: He probably means 'cogitation', i.e. thought.

7 **bastard**: 1 mixed; 2 with nothing to justify it; 3 that you are illegitimate (not Skylock's daughter)
neither: anyway

9–10 **got you not**: was not your real father
11–12 **the sins ... me**: I should be punished for my mother's sins

14–15 **Scylla ... Charybdis**: In Greek mythology, they were a monster and whirlpool that sailors had to steer between.

15 **gone**: ruined / damned
20 **enow**: enough
e'en: just

20–1 **well ... another**: live happily side by side

21–2 **raise ... hogs**: i.e. because Christians eat pork and Jews do not

23 **for money**: at any price / whatever we pay

28–9 **are out**: have fallen out

Belmont: the gardens.

Enter LANCELOT *and* JESSICA.

LANCELOT	– Yes, truly – for look you, the sins of the father are to be laid upon the children. Therefore, I promise you, I fear you. I was always plain with you, and so now I speak my agitation of the matter. Therefore be of good cheer, for truly I think you are damned.There is but one **5** hope in it that can do you any good, and that is but a kind of bastard hope neither.
JESSICA	And what hope is that, I pray thee?
LANCELOT	Marry, you may partly hope that your father got you not – that you are not the Jew's daughter. **10**
JESSICA	That were a kind of bastard hope indeed – so the sins of my *mother* should be visited upon me.
LANCELOT	Truly, then I fear you are damned both by father and mother – thus when I shun Scylla, your father, I fall into Charybdis, your mother. Well, you are gone both **15** ways.
JESSICA	I shall be saved by my husband. He hath made me a Christian.
LANCELOT	Truly, the more to blame he. We were Christians enow before – e'en as many as could well live one by **20** another. This making of Christians will raise the price of hogs – if we grow all to be pork-eaters, we shall not shortly have a rasher on the coals for money.

Enter LORENZO.

JESSICA	I'll tell my husband, Lancelot, what you say: here he comes. **25**
LORENZO	I shall grow jealous of you shortly, Lancelot, if you thus get my wife into corners.
JESSICA	Nay, you need not fear us, Lorenzo. Lancelot and I are out. He tells me flatly there's no mercy for me in heaven

Lancelot brushes off Lorenzo's accusation that he has got a black servant pregnant and, after deliberately misunderstanding Lorenzo's instructions, goes in to arrange the serving of dinner.

THINK ABOUT for GCSE

Relationships

- Look back at the earlier scenes in which Jessica and Lancelot appeared together (Act 2 Scenes 3 and 5). Considering those scenes and this one, how would you describe their relationship? Are Lancelot's comments here light-hearted or serious? How does Jessica seem to take them?

Themes and issues

- **Hatred and prejudice**: Lorenzo accuses Lancelot of having got a black girl pregnant (lines 33 to 35). How do you react to his reply, in which he plays on the words 'Moor' and 'more' (lines 36 to 38)? Is this a further example of racial prejudice in the play? Do you think this girl is mentioned only for the sake of a joke?

31 **the commonwealth**: society / the state

34 **getting … belly** making the black girl pregnant

34–5 **Moor is with child**: black African / Arab is pregnant

36 **much**: appropriate
more than reason: bigger than she should be (pun)

37 **honest**: chaste

39–40 **best grace**: most valued quality

40 **discourse**: conversation

41 **commendable**: praiseworthy

42 **sirrah**: sir (to a male servant)

43 **stomachs**: appetites

46 **'cover'** 1 lay the table; 2 wear a hat
word: correct expression

48 **I know my duty**: it would be wrong for me to keep my hat on in your presence

49 **quarrelling with occasion**: taking everything in the wrong sense / finding a double meaning in everything

56 **as humours … govern**: as the fancy takes you

57 **O dear discretion**: What fine judgement
suited: adapted / twisted to suit his meaning

60 **stand in better place**: have a better job / are higher in rank

61 **Garnished**: 1 fancily dressed; 2 provided with fancy words
tricksy: ambiguous

62 **Defy the matter**: confuse the meaning / business
How cheer'st thou: How are you

	because I am a Jew's daughter – and he says you are no good member of the commonwealth, for in converting Jews to Christians you raise the price of pork.	**30**
LORENZO	I shall answer that better to the commonwealth than you can the getting up of the Negro's belly: the Moor is with child by you, Lancelot.	**35**
LANCELOT	It is much that the Moor should be more than reason – but if she be less than an honest woman, she is indeed more than I took her for.	
LORENZO	How every fool can play upon the word! I think the best grace of wit will shortly turn into silence, and discourse grow commendable in none only but parrots. Go in, sirrah – bid them prepare for dinner.	**40**
LANCELOT	That is done, sir: they have all stomachs.	
LORENZO	Goodly Lord, what a wit-snapper are you! Then bid them *prepare* dinner.	**45**
LANCELOT	That is done too, sir – only 'cover' is the word.	
LORENZO	Will you cover then, sir?	
LANCELOT	Not so, sir, neither. I know my duty.	
LORENZO	Yet more quarrelling with occasion! Wilt thou show the whole wealth of thy wit in an instant? I pray thee understand a plain man in his plain meaning: go to thy fellows, bid them cover the table, serve in the meat, and we will come in to dinner.	**50**
LANCELOT	For the table, sir, it shall be served in. For the meat, sir, it shall be covered. For your coming in to dinner, sir, why, let it be as humours and conceits shall govern.	**55**

Exit.

LORENZO	O dear discretion, how his words are suited!
	The fool hath planted in his memory
	An army of good words, and I do know
	A many fools that stand in better place,	**60**
	Garnished like him, that for a tricksy word
	Defy the matter. How cheer'st thou, Jessica?

Jessica tells Lorenzo how much
she admires Portia and they go
in to dinner, joking with each
other.

65 **Past all expressing**: Beyond words
    meet: fitting
66 **upright**: virtuous

70 **In reason**: it stands to reason
72 **on the wager lay**: the bet was on

74 **Pawned**: staked (i.e. as part of the bet)
    rude: unrefined
75 **fellow**: equal
    Even: Just

78 **anon**: very soon

79 **a stomach**: the appetite for it

81 **howsome'er thou speak'st**: however you
    speak / whatever you say about me
82 **digest**: 1 digest like food; 2 understand
    set you forth: 1 describe; 2 praise
    highly; 3 dish up (like a meal)

THINK ABOUT for GCSE

Characterisation

• What is Jessica's opinion of
  Portia (lines 65 to 75)? What
  might have caused her to
  form such an opinion?

Relationships

• What has this scene added
  to your understanding of
  the relationship between
  Jessica and Lorenzo?
  What evidence is there to
  support the view that they
  are perfectly happy? Does
  anything suggest that there
  is still some tension in the
  relationship?

And now, good sweet, say thy opinion:
How dost thou like the Lord Bassanio's wife?

JESSICA	Past all expressing. It is very meet	65
The Lord Bassanio live an upright life –
For, having such a blessing in his lady,
He finds the joys of heaven here on earth,
And if on earth he do not merit it,
In reason he should never come to heaven.	70
Why, if two gods should play some heavenly match,
And on the wager lay two earthly women,
And Portia one, there must be something else
Pawned with the other – for the poor rude world
Hath not her fellow.

LORENZO	 Even such a husband	75
Hast thou of me, as she is for a wife.

JESSICA	Nay, but ask my opinion too of that.

LORENZO	I will anon. First, let us go to dinner.

JESSICA	Nay, let me praise you while I have a stomach.

LORENZO	No, pray thee, let it serve for table-talk –	80
Then, howsome'er thou speak'st, 'mong other things
I shall digest it.

JESSICA	 Well, I'll set you forth.

They go in together.

In this scene ...

• In court, Shylock refuses appeals to show mercy and pursues his demand for a pound of Antonio's flesh.

• Portia arrives, disguised as a young lawyer, to try the case and uses Venetian law to prevent Shylock killing Antonio.

• Bassanio is persuaded to give up the ring Portia gave him, as a reward for the young lawyer.

Antonio presents himself before the court and the Duke expresses his sympathy for him. When Shylock enters the Duke tries to persuade him to show Antonio mercy.

2 **Ready**: Present (and prepared)

3 **answer**: defend yourself against

4 **stony adversary**: hard-hearted enemy

5 **uncapable of**: unable to feel
   void: empty

6 **From any dram**: of even a tiny amount

7–8 **qualify ... course**: lessen the harshness of his intentions

8 **stands obdurate**: remains unmoved

10 **envy's**: malice's

13 **tyranny**: cruel power

THINK ABOUT for GCSE

Structure and form

• What do we assume has happened since the last time we saw Shylock and Antonio (Act 3 Scene 3)?

Performance and staging

• How do you imagine the opening of the scene in court to look like? What does the courtroom look like? Where are the characters placed?

18 **thou ... malice**: you are only keeping up your malicious behaviour

19 **last hour of act**: last moment / eleventh hour

20–1 **strange ... strange**: surprising ... unnatural

22 **exacts**: demand

24 **loose the forfeiture**: release him from paying the penalty

26 **moiety of the principal**: part of the original sum he borrowed

ACT 4   SCENE 1

Venice: the Court of Law.

Enter the DUKE OF VENICE, *with leading Citizens, Lawyers and Attendants.*

ANTONIO *is brought in, followed by* BASSANIO, GRATIANO *and* SALERIO.

DUKE	What, is Antonio here?
ANTONIO	Ready, so please your Grace.
DUKE	I am sorry for thee. Thou art come to answer
	A stony adversary, an inhuman wretch,
	Uncapable of pity, void and empty
	From any dram of mercy.

ANTONIO	I have heard
	Your Grace hath ta'en great pains to qualify
	His rigorous course. But since he stands obdurate,
	And that no lawful means can carry me
	Out of his envy's reach, I do oppose
	My patience to his fury, and am armed
	To suffer with a quietness of spirit
	The very tyranny and rage of his.

DUKE	Go one, and call the Jew into the court.
SALERIO	He is ready at the door: he comes, my lord.

Enter SHYLOCK.

DUKE	Make room, and let him stand before our face.
	– Shylock, the world thinks, and I think so too,
	That thou but lead'st this fashion of thy malice
	To the last hour of act, and then 'tis thought
	Thou'lt show thy mercy and remorse, more strange
	Than is thy strange apparent cruelty.
	And where thou now exacts the penalty,
	Which is a pound of this poor merchant's flesh,
	Thou wilt not only loose the forfeiture
	But, touched with human gentleness and love,
	Forgive a moiety of the principal,

5

10

15

20

25

Shylock rejects the Duke's pleas for mercy and explains why he is pursuing the case: he has sworn an oath to exact the penalty, he says, and he expresses his hatred for Antonio.

THINK ABOUT for GCSE

Themes and issues

• **Law, justice and mercy**: In what ways do the Duke's opening words to Shylock help us understand the difference between justice and mercy in his opinion? What do you think of the Duke's pun, 'We all expect a gentle [gentile] answer, Jew'?

Characterisation

• What does Shylock's opening speech to the court (lines 35 to 62) reveal about his motives in enforcing the bond against Antonio? Does it make him a more sympathetic character or less, in your opinion?

28 **of late**: recently
29 **Enow**: enough
    royal merchant: merchant prince
30 **commiseration of his state**: pity for his situation
31 **brassy bosoms**: hard-hearted people
32 **Turks, and Tartars**: non-Christians (then classed with Jews as pitiless unbelievers)
33 **offices**: duties
    courtesy: civilised behaviour
34 **gentle**: kind (with a probable play on 'gentile', i.e. non-Jew)
35 **possessed**: notified / informed
36 **Sabbath**: the Jewish holy day
37 **due and forfeit**: penalty now due
38 **danger light**: damage fall
39 **charter**: city's privileges
41 **carrion**: rotting
43 **my humour**: the way I am / a whim of mine / the mood I'm in
46 **baned**: poisoned
47 **gaping**: roasted with its mouth open
49 **sings i' th' nose**: makes a whining, nasal sound
50 **affection**: a strong personal response
51 **Master of passion**: controller of our most powerful emotions
53 **firm**: good
    rendered: given
54–6 **he … he …**: one person … another person …
55 **necessary**: useful
56 **of force**: involuntarily / despite anything he can do
57 **Must … shame**: has to give in to the humiliation
58 **offend**: i.e. wet himself
60 **lodged**: deep-rooted / fixed
    certain: definite / steadfast
62 **losing suit**: unprofitable case
64 **current**: course

Glancing an eye of pity on his losses
That have of late so huddled on his back
Enow to press a royal merchant down,
And pluck commiseration of his state   30
From brassy bosoms and rough hearts of flint –
From stubborn Turks, and Tartars never trained
To offices of tender courtesy.
We all expect a gentle answer, Jew.

SHYLOCK I have possessed your Grace of what I purpose,   35
And by our holy Sabbath have I sworn
To have the due and forfeit of my bond.
If you deny it, let the danger light
Upon your charter and your city's freedom!
You'll ask me why I rather choose to have   40
A weight of carrion flesh than to receive
Three thousand ducats. I'll not answer that,
But say it is my humour – is it answered?
What if my house be troubled with a rat,
And I be pleased to give ten thousand ducats   45
To have it baned? What, are you answered yet?
Some men there are love not a gaping pig;
Some that are mad if they behold a cat –
And others, when the bagpipe sings i' th' nose,
Cannot contain their urine. For affection,   50
Master of passion, sways it to the mood
Of what it likes or loathes. Now for your answer.
As there is no firm reason to be rendered
Why *he* cannot abide a gaping pig –
Why *he* a harmless necessary cat –   55
Why *he* a woollen bagpipe – but of force
Must yield to such inevitable shame
As to offend, himself being offended –
So can I give no reason, nor I will not,
More than a lodged hate and a certain loathing   60
I bear Antonio, that I follow thus
A losing suit against him. Are you answered?

BASSANIO This is no answer, thou unfeeling man,
To excuse the current of thy cruelty.

SHYLOCK I am not bound to please thee with my answers!   65

Antonio declares that it is
pointless trying to persuade
Shylock to show mercy, and
asks for the case to go ahead.
Shylock rejects Bassanio's offer
of twice the sum owed and
argues that his demand for a
pound of Antonio's flesh is a just
one.

67 **Hates ... kill?** Do you let something live
if you hate it?
68 **offence**: offence taken

70 **think you**: do you imagine you can
question: debate
72 **main flood**: high tide
bate: decrease
73 **use question**: debate

76 **wag**: sway
77 **fretten**: irritated / disturbed (fretted)

THINK ABOUT for GCSE

Language

- How does the exchange
of short speeches, such as
the one between Shylock
and Bassanio (lines 65
to 69), help here to give
the impression of a tense
and dramatic courtroom
confrontation?

Themes and issues

- **Hatred and prejudice**: In
Antonio's speech (lines 70
to 83) he uses the words 'the
Jew' or 'Jewish' three times.
Is this speech anti-Semitic?
In other words, is Antonio
suggesting that Shylock is
hard-hearted and vengeful
because he is a Jew?

82 **with ... conveniency**: being as brief and
as clear as you can

87 **draw**: take

88 **rendering**: giving

92 **abject**: low / menial
parts: tasks

96 **palates**: taste buds
97 **such viands**: food like yours

101 **fie ... law!**: your law is worthless!

BASSANIO	Do all men kill the things they do not love?
SHYLOCK	Hates any man the thing he would not kill?
BASSANIO	Every offence is not a hate at first!
SHYLOCK	What! Wouldst thou have a serpent sting thee twice?

ANTONIO I pray you, think you question with the Jew –   **70**
You may as well go stand upon the beach
And bid the main flood bate his usual height.
You may as well use question with the wolf
Why he hath made the ewe bleat for the lamb;
You may as well forbid the mountain pines   **75**
To wag their high tops and to make no noise
When they are fretten with the gusts of heaven.
You may as well do anything most hard
As seek to soften that – than which what's harder? –
His Jewish heart. Therefore, I do beseech you,   **80**
Make no more offers, use no farther means,
But with all brief and plain conveniency
Let me have judgement, and the Jew his will.

BASSANIO For thy three thousand ducats, here is six!

SHYLOCK If every ducat in six thousand ducats   **85**
Were in six parts, and every part a ducat,
I would not draw them. I would have my bond!

DUKE How shalt thou hope for mercy, rendering none?

SHYLOCK What judgement shall I dread, doing no wrong?
You have among you many a purchased slave,   **90**
Which, like your asses and your dogs and mules,
You use in abject and in slavish parts
Because you bought them. Shall I say to you
'Let them be free! Marry them to your heirs –
Why sweat they under burdens? Let their beds   **95**
Be made as soft as yours, and let their palates
Be seasoned with such viands' – ? You will answer
'The slaves are ours.' So do I answer you.
The pound of flesh which I demand of him
Is dearly bought – 'tis mine, and I will have it.   **100**
If you deny me, fie upon your law! –

Antonio is resigned to his death. Nerissa arrives, disguised as a lawyer's clerk, with a letter for the Duke from Dr Bellario, Portia's cousin. Gratiano expresses his disgust at Shylock, who is sharpening his knife in preparation for cutting off the flesh.

102 **decrees**: laws

104 **Upon … may**: It is within my powers to
106 **determine**: resolve / settle

107 **here stays without**: there is waiting outside
109 **New come**: recently arrived

113 **Ere**: before
114 **tainted**: sick
    wether: male sheep (especially a castrated ram)
115 **Meetest**: most suitable / the best one to choose
118 **epitaph**: words written about someone after their death / inscription on a grave

THINK ABOUT for GCSE

Context

• Venetian Christians sometimes owned slaves. How does Shylock use the slavery argument against the Christians to justify his demand for Antonio's flesh (lines 89 to 103)?

Characterisation

• What view does Antonio have of himself? Look at his speech (lines 114 to 118) in which he calls himself 'a tainted wether', 'meetest for death', and 'the weakest kind of fruit'. What might account for this self-image?

121 **whet**: sharpen

122 **forfeiture**: penalty

123 **sole**: i.e. of his shoe
124 **keen**: sharp
125 **hangman's**: executioner's
126 **envy**: malice / hatred

127 **wit**: intelligence
128 **inexecrable**: unspeakably detestable
129 **for … accused**: 1 let justice execute you, even if wrongly; 2 it is an injustice that you have lived this long

	There is no force in the decrees of Venice. I stand for judgement. Answer – shall I have it?	
DUKE	Upon my power I may dismiss this court, Unless Bellario, a learned doctor, Whom I have sent for to determine this, Come here today.	105
SALERIO	My lord, here stays without A messenger with letters from the doctor, New come from Padua.	
DUKE	Bring us the letters. Call the messenger!	110
BASSANIO	Good cheer, Antonio! What, man, courage yet! The Jew shall have my flesh, blood, bones and all, Ere thou shalt lose for me one drop of blood.	
ANTONIO	I am a tainted wether of the flock, Meetest for death. The weakest kind of fruit Drops earliest to the ground, and so let me. You cannot better be employed, Bassanio, Than to live still and write mine epitaph.	115

Enter NERISSA (*in disguise as a lawyer's clerk*).

| **DUKE** | Came you from Padua, from Bellario? | |
| **NERISSA** | From both, my lord. Bellario greets your Grace. | 120 |

She presents a letter to the DUKE.

BASSANIO	(*To* SHYLOCK) Why dost thou whet thy knife so earnestly?	
SHYLOCK	To cut the forfeiture from that bankrupt there.	
GRATIANO	Not on thy sole, but on thy soul, harsh Jew, Thou mak'st thy knife keen. But no metal can – No, not the hangman's axe – bear half the keenness Of thy sharp envy. Can *no* prayers pierce thee?	125
SHYLOCK	No – none that thou hast wit enough to make.	
GRATIANO	O, be thou damned, inexecrable dog! – And for thy life let justice be accused! Thou almost mak'st me waver in my faith –	130

Shylock remains unmoved by Gratiano's insults. The Duke reads out Bellario's letter: he is ill, but in his place he recommends a young lawyer called Balthazar who understands all about the case.

133 **trunks**: bodies
      currish: dog-like / mongrel
135 **fell**: deadly
      fleet: fly out
136 **unhallowed dam**: cursed mother
137 **Infused itself in**: seeped into / was absorbed into
139 **rail**: insultingly rant
140 **but offend'st**: only harm

142 **cureless**: beyond repair

143 **doth commend**: recommends

145 **attendeth ... by**: is waiting just outside

148 **conduct**: escort

THINK ABOUT *for* GCSE

Context

* Accusing Shylock (lines 130 to 138), Gratiano refers to a belief of the ancient Greek Pythagoras that the human soul might have been in an animal in another life. Shylock's soul, he claims, 'governed a wolf'. How does this help you to understand Gratiano's accusation?

Characterisation

* What impression does the letter (lines 149 to 164) give of 'Balthazar'?

152 **in loving visitation**: on a friendly visit
154 **cause in controversy**: case being disputed
156 **furnished**: equipped
157 **bettered**: improved
159 **importunity**: urging / urgent request
159–60 **fill ... stead**: take my place in answer to your Grace's summons
160 **beseech**: beg
160–1 **let his lack ... estimation**: don't fail to give him respect just because he is young
163 **trial**: 1 efforts in the case; 2 test you put him through
164 **publish his commendation**: show / spread his good reputation

To hold opinion with Pythagoras
That souls of animals infuse themselves
Into the trunks of men. Thy currish spirit
Governed a wolf, who, hanged for human slaughter,
Even from the gallows did his fell soul fleet,   **135**
And, whilst thou layest in thy unhallowed dam,
Infused itself in thee – for thy desires
Are wolvish, bloody, starved, and ravenous!

SHYLOCK   Till thou canst rail the seal from off my bond,
Thou but offend'st thy lungs to speak so loud.   **140**
Repair thy wit, good youth, or it will fall
To cureless ruin. I stand here for *law*.

DUKE   This letter from Bellario doth commend
A young and learnèd doctor to our court.
Where is he?

NERISSA   He attendeth here hard by   **145**
To know your answer, whether you'll admit him.

DUKE   With all my heart. Some three or four of you
Go give him courteous conduct to this place.

                              Exit a Lawyer, with Attendants.

– Meantime the court shall hear Bellario's letter.
(*He reads.*) 'Your Grace shall understand that at the   **150**
receipt of your letter I am very sick, but in the instant
that your messenger came, in loving visitation was with
me a young doctor of Rome. His name is Balthazar. I
acquainted him with the cause in controversy between
the Jew and Antonio the merchant; we turned o'er   **155**
many books together. He is furnished with my opinion,
which, bettered with his own learning, the greatness
whereof I cannot enough commend, comes with him
at my importunity, to fill up your Grace's request in
my stead. I beseech you let his lack of years be no   **160**
impediment to let him lack a reverend estimation, for I
never knew so young a body with so old a head. I leave
him to your gracious acceptance, whose trial shall
better publish his commendation.'

Portia enters, disguised as the lawyer Balthazar. She opens the case by asking Shylock to be merciful. She explains the true nature of mercy.

THINK ABOUT for GCSE

Performance and staging

- Portia asks, 'Which is the merchant here – and which the Jew?' (line 172). What effect might that question have if Shylock and Antonio are dressed (a) similarly or (b) very differently?

Themes and issues

- **Law, justice and mercy**: Portia's first exchange with the Duke and Shylock is full of legal terms. What are the exact meanings of: 'difference' (line 169), 'question' (line 170), 'cause' (line 171), 'suit' (line 175), 'cannot impugn you' (line 177), 'You stand within his danger' (line 178) and 'confess the bond' (line 179)?

Language

- What is the effect of all this legal language?

169 **difference**: dispute
170 **present question**: current argument / case
171 **throughly**: thoroughly
    cause: case

175 **suit you follow**: case you bring
176 **in such rule**: you have followed the law so correctly
177 **impugn**: oppose / challenge
178 **within his danger**: at his mercy / within his power to harm you

181 **On … must I?**: What can force me?
182 **strained**: 1 compelled; 2 complicated; 3 filtered, like rainwater
184 **is twice blest**: bestows a double blessing
186 **mightiest in the mightiest**: most effective in the most powerful
    becomes: suits
188 **shows**: represents
    temporal: earthly
189 **attribute to**: quality of

PORTIA (*in disguise as 'Balthazar', the young doctor of law*) *is brought in.*

	– You hear the learn'd Bellario what he writes.	**165**
	– And here, I take it, is the doctor come.	
	(*To* PORTIA) Give me your hand. Came you from old	
	Bellario?	

PORTIA   I did, my lord.

DUKE   You are welcome. Take your place.
Are you acquainted with the difference
That holds this present question in the court?   **170**

PORTIA   I am informèd throughly of the cause.
Which is the merchant here – and which the Jew?

DUKE   Antonio and old Shylock, both stand forth.

PORTIA   Is your name Shylock?

SHYLOCK   Shylock is my name.

PORTIA   Of a strange nature is the suit you follow,   **175**
Yet in such rule that the Venetian law
Cannot impugn you as you do proceed.
– (*To* ANTONIO) You stand within his danger, do you
    not?

ANTONIO   Ay, so he says.

PORTIA   Do you confess the bond?

ANTONIO   I do.

PORTIA   Then must the Jew be merciful.   **180**

SHYLOCK   On what compulsion must I? Tell me that.

PORTIA   The quality of mercy is not strained –
It droppeth as the gentle rain from heaven
Upon the place beneath. It is twice blest:
It blesseth him that gives, and him that takes.   **185**
'Tis mightiest in the mightiest: it becomes
The thronèd monarch better than his crown.
His sceptre shows the force of temporal power,
The attribute to awe and majesty,

Portia reminds Shylock that mercy is powerful, and is the only thing that can save people from damnation. But Shylock refuses to budge. When Bassanio asks the Duke to bend the law to save Antonio, Portia objects, saying that to do so would have a harmful effect on future cases. At this, Shylock praises her skill as a lawyer.

THINK ABOUT for GCSE

Themes and issues

* **Law, justice and mercy**: What, according to Portia, is 'the quality of mercy' (line 182)? How does she define it? What distinction does she draw between 'justice' and 'mercy'? How should they be connected?

Characterisation

* Portia has explained the workings of mercy to Shylock, then offers him three times the money owed (line 225). Is she genuinely trying to persuade him to withdraw his claim over Antonio or is this part of a clever ruse to catch him out?

---

190 **dread and fear**: reverence and awe
191 **sway**: rule

194 **doth … likest**: then most closely resembles
195 **seasons**: softens / modifies
197 **justice**: 1 passing judgements; 2 under God's justice
198 **see salvation**: be saved
199 **render**: perform in return
201 **mitigate … plea**: soften / moderate that part of your plea that asks only for justice
203 **Must needs**: will have to
204 **My … head!** I accept the consequences of my actions!
     crave: demand
206 **discharge**: pay back
207 **tender**: offer

211 **must appear**: will be evident
212 **malice … truth**: hatred is defeating what is right
213 **Wrest … authority**: use your official power to bend the law just once
215 **curb**: restrain / hold back

217 **decree establishèd**: law which already exists
218 **for a precedent**: as an example when judging future cases

221 **Daniel**: Like Portia, Daniel in the Bible was young and gave a correct judgement.

225 **thrice**: three times

	Wherein doth sit the dread and fear of kings –	190

Wherein doth sit the dread and fear of kings –   190
But mercy is above this sceptred sway.
It is enthronèd in the hearts of kings:
It is an attribute to God himself –
And earthly power doth then show likest God's
When mercy seasons justice. Therefore, Jew,   195
Though justice be thy plea, consider this:
That in the course of justice none of us
Should see salvation. We do pray for mercy,
And that same prayer doth teach us all to render
The deeds of mercy. I have spoke thus much   200
To mitigate the justice of thy plea,
Which, if thou follow, this strict court of Venice
Must needs give sentence 'gainst the merchant there.

SHYLOCK   My deeds upon my head! I crave the law –
The penalty and forfeit of my bond.   205

PORTIA   Is he not able to discharge the money?

BASSANIO   Yes, here I tender it for him in the court –
Yea, twice the sum. If that will not suffice,
I will be bound to pay it ten times o'er
On forfeit of my hands, my head, my heart.   210
If this will not suffice, it must appear
That malice bears down truth. And I beseech you
Wrest once the law to your authority –
To do a great right, do a little wrong,
And curb this cruel devil of his will!   215

PORTIA   It must not be. There is no power in Venice
Can alter a decree establishèd.
'Twill be recorded for a precedent,
And many an error by the same example
Will rush into the state. It cannot be.   220

SHYLOCK   A Daniel come to judgement! – Yea, a Daniel!
O wise young judge, how I do honour thee!

PORTIA   I pray you let me look upon the bond.

SHYLOCK   Here 'tis, most reverend doctor, here it is.

PORTIA   Shylock, there's thrice thy money offered thee.   225

Shylock now turns down an offer of three times the money owed him and refuses to listen to further arguments. Portia tells Antonio to prepare himself. Shylock has a set of scales at hand to weigh out the flesh.

227 perjury: oath-breaking / lying under oath

228 this bond is forfeit: i.e. Antonio has to pay the penalty

233 tenor: exact wording

235 exposition: explanation
236 charge: order / ask
237 pillar: upholder / supporter

240 alter me: make me change my mind
stay: stand firm / take my stand
241 beseech: beg

246 Hath full relation to: fully authorise

THINK ABOUT
for GCSE

Themes and issues

* **Truth and deception**: What does Shylock mean by 'Shall I lay perjury on my soul?' (lines 226 to 228)? Is he being genuine in claiming that he has 'an oath in heaven', or hypocritical, in your opinion?

253 balance: a set of scales

SHYLOCK	An oath, an oath! – I have an oath in heaven! –
	Shall I lay perjury upon my soul?
	No, not for Venice.

PORTIA   Why, this bond is forfeit –
And lawfully by this the Jew may claim
A pound of flesh, to be by him cut off   **230**
Nearest the merchant's heart. (*To* SHYLOCK) Be
    merciful –
Take thrice thy money. Bid me tear the bond.

SHYLOCK When it is paid, according to the tenor.
It doth appear you are a worthy judge:
You know the law; your exposition   **235**
Hath been most sound. I charge you *by* the law,
Whereof you are a well-deserving pillar,
Proceed to judgement. By my soul I swear,
There is no power in the tongue of man
To alter me. I stay here on my bond.   **240**

ANTONIO Most heartily I do beseech the court
To give the judgement.

PORTIA   Why then, thus it is:
You must prepare your bosom for his knife.

SHYLOCK O noble judge! O excellent young man!

PORTIA For the intent and purpose of the law   **245**
Hath full relation to the penalty
Which here appeareth due upon the bond.

SHYLOCK 'Tis very true. O wise and upright judge,
How much more elder art thou than thy looks!

PORTIA (*To* ANTONIO) Therefore lay bare your bosom.

SHYLOCK   Ay – his breast –   **250**
So says the bond, doth it not, noble judge?
'Nearest his heart' – those are the very words.

PORTIA It is so. Are there balance here to weigh
The flesh?

SHYLOCK   I have them ready.

Portia requests that Shylock have a surgeon stand by. Antonio takes a loving farewell of Bassanio, claiming to be glad that he will not have to live on in poverty. He asks that Portia should be told about his love for Bassanio.

THINK ABOUT for GCSE

Characterisation

- What do Antonio's words to Bassanio (lines 262 to 279) reveal about his present attitude to life, his love for Bassanio and the love he assumes Bassanio has for him?

Performance and staging

- How might Antonio deliver this farewell speech to Bassanio? Think about tone of voice, gestures, facial expressions, pauses and movements.

- In performance, what are the effects of Portia's and Nerissa's comments on their husbands' 'offers' here (lines 286 to 287 and 291 to 292)?

---

255 **on your charge**: at your expense / on your responsibility

257 **nominated**: specified / stated

259 **'Twere**: It would be
for charity: out of human kindness

262 **armed**: fortified / steeled

266 **still her use**: always her way

269 **age**: old age
ling'ring penance: drawn-out punishment
272 **the process … end**: the manner of Antonio's death
273 **speak me fair**: speak well of me
275 **love**: lover / friend
276 **Repent but you**: Only be sorry

279 **with all my heart**: 1 most willingly; 2 (literally)

283 **esteemed**: valued
284 **ay**: yes

288 **protest**: declare

290 **currish**: dog-like / evil dog of a

PORTIA	Have by some surgeon, Shylock, on your charge,	255
	To stop his wounds, lest he do bleed to death.	
SHYLOCK	Is it so nominated in the bond?	
PORTIA	It is not so expressed, but what of that?	
	'Twere good you do so much for charity.	
SHYLOCK	I cannot find it – 'tis not in the bond.	260
PORTIA	(*To* ANTONIO) You, merchant: have you anything to say?	
ANTONIO	But little – I am armed and well prepared.	
	Give me your hand, Bassanio. Fare you well.	
	Grieve not that I am fall'n to this for you –	
	For herein Fortune shows herself more kind	265
	Than is her custom. It is still her use	
	To let the wretched man outlive his wealth,	
	To view with hollow eye and wrinkled brow	
	An age of poverty – from which ling'ring penance	
	Of such misery doth she cut me off.	270
	Commend me to your honourable wife.	
	Tell her the process of Antonio's end,	
	Say how I loved you, speak me fair in death –	
	And when the tale is told, bid her be judge	
	Whether Bassanio had not once a love.	275
	Repent but you that you shall lose your friend	
	And he repents not that he pays your debt.	
	For if the Jew do cut but deep enough,	
	I'll pay it instantly, with all my heart.	
BASSANIO	Antonio, I am married to a wife	280
	Which is as dear to me as life itself –	
	But life itself, my wife, and all the world,	
	Are not with me esteemed above thy life.	
	I would lose all, ay, sacrifice them all	
	Here to this devil, to deliver you.	285
PORTIA	Your wife would give you little thanks for that	
	If she were by to hear you make the offer.	
GRATIANO	*I* have a wife who I protest *I* love –	
	I would she were in heaven, so she could	
	Entreat some power to change this currish Jew!	290

Portia gives the judgement in Shylock's favour, but, just as he is about to use his knife on Antonio, she stops him. Shylock can take the flesh, but if he sheds one drop of blood, all his lands and goods will be forfeited. Shylock backs down and declares that he is willing to accept the offer of three times the money owed him. But Portia stands firm – he must take the flesh and accept the consequences.

THINK ABOUT for GCSE

Context

- In the Bible, the Jews chose to release Barrabas the thief from crucifixion instead of Jesus. How does the Barrabas reference help to express the force of Shylock's feelings (lines 293 to 296)? What might he be implying about Lorenzo?

Characterisation

- From what you know of Portia's plans and behaviour so far, has she had the 'jot of blood' idea in her head all along (line 304) or does it occur to her only at the last minute?

291 **'Tis well**: It's just as well
292 **else**: otherwise

294 **stock of Barrabas**: offspring of the thief set free instead of Jesus
296 **trifle**: waste
     pursue: proceed with

303 **Tarry a little**: Wait a moment
304 **jot**: drop

312 **act**: law as it is written down

316 **thrice**: three times

318 **Soft!**: Wait a moment! / Not so fast!

NERISSA	'Tis well you offer it behind her back – The wish would make else an unquiet house.
SHYLOCK	These be the Christian husbands! I have a daughter – Would any of the stock of Barrabas Had been her husband, rather than a Christian! **295** We trifle time – I pray thee pursue sentence.
PORTIA	A pound of that same merchant's flesh is thine. The court awards it, and the law doth give it.
SHYLOCK	Most rightful judge!
PORTIA	And you must cut this flesh from off his breast. **300** The law allows it, and the court awards it.
SHYLOCK	Most learnèd judge! A sentence! – Come, prepare!
PORTIA	Tarry a little. There is something else. This bond doth give thee here no jot of blood: The words expressly are 'a pound of flesh'. **305** Take then thy bond, take thou thy pound of flesh, But in the cutting it, if thou doth shed One drop of Christian blood, thy lands and goods Are by the laws of Venice confiscate Unto the state of Venice.
GRATIANO	O upright judge! **310** Mark, Jew – O learnèd judge!
SHYLOCK	Is that the law?
PORTIA	Thyself shalt see the act. For as thou urgest justice, be assured Thou shalt have justice more than thou desir'st.
GRATIANO	O learnèd judge! Mark, Jew, a learnèd judge! **315**
SHYLOCK	I take this offer then. Pay the bond thrice And let the Christian go.
BASSANIO	Here is the money.
PORTIA	Soft! The Jew shall have all justice – soft, no haste! He shall have nothing but the penalty. **320**

Portia adds a further condition: Shylock has to take exactly a pound. Defeated, Shylock tries to leave but Portia stops him with another law: if a foreigner plots to kill a Venetian, half his wealth can be confiscated by the state and the other half given to the intended victim. He can also be executed.

325 a just pound: exactly a pound
326 substance: amount / weight

328 scruple: (a tiny quantity)

THINK ABOUT for GCSE

Language

• Some people consider Portia's legal points about the 'jot of blood' (lines 304 to 310) and 'just a pound' (lines 323 to 330) to be nothing more than clever playing with words. What justification might Shylock have in feeling that he has been cheated?

• What is the meaning of the word 'alien' in this context (line 347)? What is its force when used against Shylock?

Characterisation

• What goes through Shylock's mind from Portia's 'Tarry a little' (line 303) to 'I'll stay no longer question' (line 344)? Trace the possible course of his thoughts and feelings.

332 infidel: unbeliever
on the hip: at my mercy / at a disadvantage (a wrestling term)
334 my principal: the basic sum I lent him (i.e. 3,000 ducats)

337 merely: 1 only; 2 absolutely

340 barely: at the very least

344 I'll … question: I'm not going to wait to argue this case any further
Tarry: Wait
347 alien: foreigner (i.e. someone not a citizen of Venice)

350 party: person
contrive: plot
351 seize: take legal possession of
352 privy coffer: private treasury
354 'gainst … voice: with no appeals allowed

Gratiano	O Jew – an upright judge! – A learnèd judge!
Portia	Therefore prepare thee to cut off the flesh. Shed thou no blood, nor cut thou less nor more But just a pound of flesh. If thou tak'st more Or less than a just pound, be it but so much 325 As makes it light or heavy in the substance Or the division of the twentieth part Of one poor scruple – nay, if the scale do turn But in the estimation of a hair, Thou diest, and all thy goods are confiscate. 330
Gratiano	A second Daniel – a Daniel, Jew! Now, infidel, I have you on the hip.
Portia	Why doth the Jew pause? Take thy forfeiture.
Shylock	Give me my principal, and let me go.
Bassanio	I have it ready for thee – here it is. 335
Portia	He hath refused it in the open court. He shall have merely justice and his bond.
Gratiano	A Daniel still say I, a second Daniel! I thank thee, Jew, for teaching me that word.
Shylock	Shall I not have barely my principal? 340
Portia	Thou shalt have nothing but the forfeiture, To be so taken at thy peril, Jew.
Shylock	Why then, the devil give him good of it! I'll stay no longer question.
Portia	Tarry, Jew. The law hath yet another hold on you. 345 It is enacted in the laws of Venice, If it be proved against an alien That by direct or indirect attempts He seek the life of any citizen, The party 'gainst the which he doth contrive 350 Shall seize one half his goods. The other half Comes to the privy coffer of the state, And the offender's life lies in the mercy Of the Duke only, 'gainst all other voice.

Shylock's life is spared. The state may not take half Shylock's money but may only fine him. Antonio is willing for Shylock not to be fined, so long as he can have control of the other half of Shylock's wealth, to give to Lorenzo when Shylock dies. But there are two conditions: that Shylock must become a Christian, and that he must make a will leaving all his possessions to Lorenzo and Jessica when he dies.

356 **by manifest proceeding**: by your clearly observed course of action
358 **contrived**: plotted
359–60 **incurred ... rehearsed**: brought upon yourself the penalty I have just described
361 **Down**: On your knees!

365 **charge**: cost
366 **our**: 1 the Duke's; 2 Christians'

368 **For**: As for
370 **humbleness**: a show of humility and remorse
     drive: reduce

374 **sustain**: support

377 **halter gratis**: noose (with which to hang himself) free of charge
379 **quit**: release Shylock from
380 **so he**: so long as he
381 **in use**: in a legal trust
     render: give

385 **presently**: immediately
386 **record a gift**: sign a legal 'deed of gift' / make a will
387 **all ... possessed**: everything he owns when he dies
388 **son**: son-in-law
389 **recant**: take back
390 **late**: just now

THINK ABOUT for GCSE

Themes and issues

- **Money and business**: What exactly are the *financial* penalties imposed on Shylock? Look first at lines 346 to 354 and 368 to 371, and then lines 379 to 383 and 386 to 388. How just are these penalties, in your opinion?

- **Law, justice and mercy**: What is your opinion of the mercy Antonio offers to Shylock (lines 376 to 388)? In particular, what is your reaction to the condition that 'he presently become a Christian' (line 385)?

	In which predicament I say thou stand'st –	355
	For it appears by manifest proceeding	
	That indirectly, and directly too,	
	Thou hast contrived against the very life	
	Of the defendant; and thou hast incurred	
	The danger formerly by me rehearsed.	360
	Down, therefore, and beg mercy of the Duke.	

GRATIANO   Beg that thou mayst have leave to hang thyself! –
           And yet, thy wealth being forfeit to the state,
           Thou hast not left the value of a cord –
           Therefore thou must be hanged at the state's charge.   365

DUKE   That thou shalt see the difference of our spirit,
           I pardon thee thy life before thou ask it.
           For half thy wealth, it is Antonio's –
           The other half comes to the general state,
           Which humbleness may drive unto a fine.   370

PORTIA   Ay, for the state – not for Antonio.

SHYLOCK   Nay, take my life and all – pardon not that.
           You take my house when you do take the prop
           That doth sustain my house. You take my life
           When you do take the means whereby I live.   375

PORTIA   What mercy can you render him, Antonio?

GRATIANO   A halter gratis – nothing else, for God's sake!

ANTONIO   So please my lord the Duke and all the court
           To quit the fine for one half of his goods,
           I am content – so he will let me have   380
           The other half in use, to render it
           Upon his death unto the gentleman
           That lately stole his daughter.
           Two things provided more: that for this favour
           He presently become a Christian;   385
           The other, that he do record a gift,
           Here in the court, of all he dies possessed
           Unto his son Lorenzo and his daughter.

DUKE   He shall do this – or else I do recant
           The pardon that I late pronouncèd here.   390

Shylock agrees to the conditions and leaves the court. The Duke thanks the disguised Portia, and Bassanio offers her the three thousand ducats that had been owed to Shylock, but she refuses.

391 Art thou contented ... ?: Do you agree ... ?

396 christening: becoming a Christian

397 ten more: i.e. to bring the number up to the twelve required to sentence him to hang (Jurymen were sometimes called 'godfathers' because they sent the condemned man to God's judgement.)

398 font: place where a Christian is baptised

399 entreat you home: beg you to come home

400 of pardon: to excuse me

402 meet ... forth: fitting that I should leave immediately

403 your ... not: you don't have the time

404 gratify: reward

405 you ... him: you owe him a great deal

408 acquitted of: released from
in lieu whereof: in return for which

410 freely ... withal: willingly give you for the trouble you have so generously taken

414 delivering: freeing

415 therein: in doing that
account: consider

416 My ... mercenary: beyond that, I am not interested in money

417 know: remember / recognise

419 of force ... further: I really must try to persuade you

420 tribute: token of our thanks

THINK ABOUT for GCSE

Performance and staging

- How might Shylock leave the courtroom (line 398)? Some actors have howled in anguish, some collapse physically, while others try to show that Shylock is only temporarily defeated and will be back.

Characterisation

- What role does Gratiano fulfil from the moment the tables are turned on Shylock through to Shylock's exit (lines 310 to 398)? What is your opinion of Gratiano here?

PORTIA	Art thou contented, Jew? What dost thou say?

PORTIA Art thou contented, Jew? What dost thou say?

SHYLOCK I am content.

PORTIA Clerk, draw a deed of gift.

SHYLOCK I pray you give me leave to go from hence.
I am not well. Send the deed after me,
And I will sign it.

DUKE Get thee gone, but do it. 395

GRATIANO In christening shalt thou have two godfathers:
Had I been judge, thou shouldst have had ten more,
To bring thee to the gallows, not to the font.

Exit SHYLOCK.

DUKE (*To* PORTIA) Sir, I entreat you home with me to dinner.

PORTIA I humbly do desire your grace of pardon: 400
I must away this night toward Padua,
And it is meet I presently set forth.

DUKE I am sorry that your leisure serves you not.
Antonio, gratify this gentleman,
For in my mind you are much bound to him. 405

Exit, followed by Citizens, Lawyers and Attendants.

BASSANIO (*To* PORTIA) Most worthy gentleman, I and my friend
Have by your wisdom been this day acquitted
Of grievous penalties, in lieu whereof
Three thousand ducats, due unto the Jew,
We freely cope your courteous pains withal. 410

ANTONIO – And stand indebted over and above
In love and service to you evermore.

PORTIA He is well paid that is well satisfied,
And I, delivering you, am satisfied,
And therein do account myself well paid: 415
My mind was never yet more mercenary.
I pray you know me when we meet again.
I wish you well, and so I take my leave.

BASSANIO Dear sir, of force I must attempt you further.
Take some remembrance of us as a tribute, 420

When pressed to accept some gift, Portia asks for Bassanio's ring – the one she had given him as a love-token – but he refuses. As soon as she has left, pretending to be offended, Antonio persuades Bassanio to give the ring to the young lawyer.

THINK ABOUT for GCSE

Language

- There is a great deal of sexual language in the exchange between Portia and Bassanio: 'satisfied' (lines 413 to 414), 'know me' (line 417), 'attempt you' (line 419), 'press me' and 'yield' (line 423), 'love' and 'deny me' (line 427). How far is this an example of dramatic irony?

Performance and staging

- What effect might this language have on the way the exchange between 'Balthazar' and Bassanio is performed, especially if one of the characters is fully aware of the sexual meanings?

422 **pardon me**: excuse me (for insisting)
423 **press me far**: are very insistent

425 **for your love**: in friendship

427 **in love**: out of generosity

428 **trifle**: of no value

431 **a mind to it**: set my heart on it
432 **depends … value**: at stake than the monetary value

434 **proclamation**: advertising for it
435 **Only for this**: but as far as this (ring) is concerned
436 **liberal in**: generous when it comes to making

442 **'scuse**: excuse

445 **hold out enemy**: persist in being your enemy

448 **withal**: as well / in addition

Not as a fee. Grant me two things, I pray you:
Not to deny me, and to pardon me.

Portia You press me far, and therefore I will yield.
(*To* Antonio) Give me your gloves – I'll wear them for your sake –
(*To* Bassanio) And, for your love, I'll take this ring from you.
Do not draw back your hand – I'll take no more,
And you in love shall not deny me this.

Bassanio This ring, good sir? Alas, it is a trifle.
I will not shame myself to give you this!

Portia I will have nothing else but only this,
And now methinks I have a mind to it.

Bassanio There's more depends on this than on the value.
The dearest ring in Venice will I give you,
And find it out by proclamation –
Only for this I pray you pardon me!

Portia I see, sir, you are liberal in offers.
You taught me first to beg, and now methinks
You teach me how a beggar should be answered.

Bassanio Good sir, this ring was given me by my wife,
And when she put it on, she made me vow
That I should neither sell, nor give, nor lose it.

Portia That 'scuse serves many men to save their gifts.
And if your wife be not a mad woman,
And know how well I have deserved this ring,
She would not hold out enemy for ever
For giving it to me. – Well, peace be with you.

Exit, with Nerissa.

Antonio My Lord Bassanio, let him have the ring.
Let his deservings, and my love withal,
Be valued 'gainst your wife's commandment.

Bassanio (*Taking off the ring*) Go, Gratiano – run and overtake him.

Bassanio plans to return
with Antonio to Belmont the
following morning.

453 thither presently: go there at once

455 Fly: hasten

THINK ABOUT
for GCSE

Characterisation

• How would you answer
someone who argued
that Portia was hard
and manipulating? She
deliberately leads Shylock
into a trap and ensures that
he is severely penalised
(lines 345 to 371). She then
torments Bassanio by putting
him in a position where he
has either to seem ungrateful
to the lawyer who has saved
his best friend's life or give
up the ring from Portia that
he has sworn to cherish
(lines 424 to 446).

Performance and staging

• How might Gratiano react
when Bassanio tells him to
give the lawyer the ring (line
450 to 452)?

Give him the ring – and bring him if thou canst
Unto Antonio's house. Away – make haste!

Exit GRATIANO.

– Come, you and I will thither presently,
And in the morning early will we both
Fly toward Belmont. Come, Antonio.   **455**

They go off together.

Act 4 Scene 2

In this scene ...

- Gratiano has run after Portia with Bassanio's ring and she politely accepts the gift.
- Nerissa decides to test Gratiano by seeing if she can get her ring from him as well.

1 **Inquire ... out**: Find out where Shylock lives
deed: i.e. the deed of gift stating that Shylock will leave his possessions to Jessica and Lorenzo
5 **you ... o'erta'en**: I'm glad I caught you
6 **upon more advice**: after further reflection / on second thoughts

THINK ABOUT for GCSE

Performance and staging

- How might Portia react when Gratiano brings her the ring (lines 5 to 11)? Might she be amused, for example, or hurt?

Themes and issues

- **Love and friendship**: From the evidence so far, what differences do you think there are in the ways the men and the women view the rings?

15 **Thou ... warrant**: I bet you'll succeed
old: plenty of

17 **outface them**: stand our ground and deny their claims
18 **tarry**: be waiting

Venice: a street.

Enter Portia *and* Nerissa.

PORTIA   Inquire the Jew's house out. Give him this deed,
              And let him sign it. We'll away tonight,
              And be a day before our husbands home.
              This deed will be well welcome to Lorenzo.

        Enter Gratiano.

GRATIANO   Fair sir – you are well o'erta'en –   5
              My Lord Bassanio upon more advice
              Hath sent you here this ring – and doth entreat
              Your company at dinner.

PORTIA   That cannot be.
              His ring I do accept most thankfully,
              And so I pray you tell him. Furthermore,   10
              I pray you show my youth old Shylock's house.

GRATIANO   That will I do.

NERISSA   Sir, I would speak with you.
              – (*Aside to* Portia) I'll see if I can get my husband's
                      ring
              Which I did make him swear to keep for ever.

PORTIA   (*Aside to* Nerissa) Thou mayst, I warrant. We shall have
                  old swearing   15
              That they did give the rings away to men –
              But we'll outface them, and outswear them too.
              (*Aloud*) Away – make haste! Thou know'st where I will
                  tarry.

                                                                Exit.

NERISSA   (*To* Gratiano) Come, good sir – will you show me to
                  this house?

                                                Exit, with Gratiano.

In this scene ...

- Lorenzo and Jessica sit in the moonlight and talk of lovers.
- Bassanio and Gratiano are accused of having given their rings away to women.
- Portia and Nerissa tease their husbands but the truth is finally revealed, and Antonio finds that some of his ships have returned safely.

At Belmont, Lorenzo and Jessica are recalling lovers from classical myths and stories, who met on moonlit nights such as this one.

7   **o'ertrip**: skip over
8   **ere himself**: before she saw the lion itself

10   **willow**: emblem of forsaken love
11   **waft**: beckoned / waved

THINK ABOUT for GCSE

Themes and issues

- **Love and friendship**: In myth, all the lovers referred to here were unhappy. Troilus the Trojan believed that his lover Cressida had betrayed him (lines 1 to 6); Pyramus and Thisby both committed suicide (lines 6 to 9); Dido was deserted by her lover Aeneas (lines 9 to 12); and Medea was deserted by Aeson's son Jason (lines 12 to 14). How do you interpret Jessica's continuation of the list of lovers (lines 17 to 20) and Lorenzo's reply (lines 20 to 22)?

14   **renew**: rejuvenate

15   **steal from**: 1 creep away from; 2 rob
16   **unthrift love**: poor / spendthrift lover

19   **vows**: promises

21   **shrew**: ill-tempered / nagging woman
22   **Slander**: tell lies about
23   **out-'night' you**: outdo you in 'In such a night ...' stories
24   **footing**: footsteps

The gardens at Belmont: after nightfall.
Enter LORENZO *and* JESSICA.

LORENZO	The moon shines bright. In such a night as this,
	When the sweet wind did gently kiss the trees
	And they did make no noise, in such a night
	Troilus methinks mounted the Trojan walls,
	And sighed his soul toward the Grecian tents 5
	Where Cressid lay that night.
JESSICA	In such a night
	Did Thisby fearfully o'ertrip the dew,
	And saw the lion's shadow ere himself,
	And ran dismayed away.
LORENZO	In such a night
	Stood Dido with a willow in her hand 10
	Upon the wild sea banks, and waft her love
	To come again to Carthage.
JESSICA	In such a night
	Medea gathered the enchanted herbs
	That did renew old Aeson.
LORENZO	In such a night
	Did Jessica steal from the wealthy Jew, 15
	And with an unthrift love did run from Venice
	As far as Belmont.
JESSICA	In such a night
	Did young Lorenzo swear he loved her well,
	Stealing her soul with many vows of faith,
	And ne'er a true one.
LORENZO	In such a night 20
	Did pretty Jessica, like a little shrew,
	Slander her love, and he forgave it her.
JESSICA	I would out-'night' you, did nobody come –
	But hark, I hear the footing of a man.

Stephano, a servant, approaches and reports that Portia is expected home before dawn. Lancelot enters to say that Bassanio will be back at about the same time.

30–1   **doth … crosses**: stops occasionally by wayside shrines
32   **wedlock**: marriage

37–8   **ceremoniously … welcome**: arrange some ceremony to welcome

THINK ABOUT for GCSE

Characterisation

• Do we assume that Portia really may have visited 'holy crosses' accompanied by 'a holy hermit' (lines 30 to 33) or is this a fiction made up by her to cover her absence?

Performance and staging

• Lancelot's entrance (line 39) often signals a change of mood. How might it be played for comic effect? For example, what does Lancelot do as he enters? How is he dressed? What noises does he make?

39   **Sola!**: (imitating the sound of a messenger's post-horn)
     Woo-ha-ho!: (imitating a falconer's call)

43   **Leave hallooing**: Stop shouting

46   **post**: messenger / courier
47   **horn**: 1 post horn; 2 'horn of plenty' filled with good things
48   **ere**: before

49   **expect**: await

51   **signify**: tell the servants

Enter STEPHANO, *a messenger.*

LORENZO	Who comes so fast in silence of the night?	**25**
STEPHANO	A friend.	
LORENZO	A friend? What friend? – Your name, I pray you, friend?	
STEPHANO	Stephano is my name, and I bring word My mistress will before the break of day Be here at Belmont. She doth stray about By holy crosses, where she kneels and prays For happy wedlock hours.	**30**
LORENZO	Who comes with her?	
STEPHANO	None but a holy hermit and her maid. I pray you, is my master yet returned?	
LORENZO	He is not, nor we have not heard from him. But go we in, I pray thee, Jessica, And ceremoniously let us prepare Some welcome for the mistress of the house.	**35**

Enter LANCELOT.

LANCELOT	Sola, sola! Woo-ha-ho! – Sola, sola!	
LORENZO	Who calls?	**40**
LANCELOT	Sola! – Did you see Master Lorenzo? – Master Lorenzo! – Sola, sola!	
LORENZO	Leave hallooing, man! – Here!	
LANCELOT	Sola! Where, where?	
LORENZO	Here!	**45**
LANCELOT	Tell him there's a post come from my master, with his horn full of good news! My master will be here ere morning.	

Exit.

LORENZO	Sweet soul, let's in, and there expect their coming. And yet no matter – why should we go in? My friend Stephano, signify, I pray you,	**50**

Lorenzo and Jessica sit watching the stars. Lorenzo asks the musicians to play and talks about the power of music.

53   **music**: Portia's band of musicians

57   **Become**: go well with
      touches: strains
58   **floor of heaven**: night sky
59   **patens**: little plates / spangles
60–1 **There's … sings**: Even the tiniest star visible makes angelic music in its orbit
62   **Still choiring**: continually singing
      young-eyed cherubins: sharp-eyed angels
64–5 **whilst … it in**: while our souls are trapped inside our mortal bodies
66   **Diana**: goddess of the moon and chastity
67   **touches**: strains of music
70   **spirits**: mental faculties / feelings
71   **do but note**: if you just look at
      wanton: uncontrolled / unrestrained
72   **race**: herd
      unhandled colts: unbroken / untamed young horses
73   **Fetching mad bounds**: leaping madly
75   **hear perchance**: happen to hear
76   **air of music**: tune
77   **make a mutual stand**: stand still together / pause together
78   **modest**: calm and controlled
79   **Therefore**: That is why
      the poet: The Roman poet Ovid told the story of Orpheus, who could charm even inanimate objects with his music.
80   **Did feign**: invented the story
      drew: could attract
      floods: rivers
81   **Since nought**: since there is nothing
      stockish: insensitive / unfeeling
82   **But … nature**: whose nature cannot be changed for a while by music
84   **concord**: harmony
85   **stratagems**: plotting violent deeds
      spoils: pillaging / plunder

THINK ABOUT for GCSE

Relationships

• What does the opening of this scene (lines 1 to 69) add to our understanding of the relationship between Jessica and Lorenzo? How happy are they? Are there any signs that Jessica might be questioning her actions in running away with Lorenzo?

Structure and form

• What is the effect of the music and Lorenzo's speeches about it (lines 55 to 88) at this point in the scene, and in the play?

Within the house, your mistress is at hand –
And bring your music forth into the air.

Exit STEPHANO.

– How sweet the moonlight sleeps upon this bank!
Here will we sit, and let the sounds of music   55
Creep in our ears. Soft stillness and the night
Become the touches of sweet harmony.
Sit, Jessica. Look how the floor of heaven
Is thick inlaid with patens of bright gold.
There's not the smallest orb which thou behold'st   60
But in his motion like an angel sings,
Still choiring to the young-eyed cherubins.
Such harmony is in immortal souls –
But whilst this muddy vesture of decay
Doth grossly close it in, we cannot hear it.   65

Re-enter STEPHANO, *bringing Portia's musicians.*

– Come, ho! – And wake Diana with a hymn!
With sweetest touches pierce your mistress' ear,
And draw her home with music.

Music is played.

JESSICA   I am never merry when I hear sweet music.

LORENZO   The reason is your spirits are attentive.   70
For do but note a wild and wanton herd
Or race of youthful and unhandled colts,
Fetching mad bounds, bellowing and neighing loud –
Which is the hot condition of their blood.
If they but hear perchance a trumpet sound,   75
Or any air of music touch their ears,
You shall perceive them make a mutual stand,
Their savage eyes turned to a modest gaze
By the sweet power of music. Therefore the poet
Did feign that Orpheus drew trees, stones, and floods –   80
Since naught so stockish, hard, and full of rage,
But music for the time doth change his nature.
The man that hath no music in himself,
Nor is not moved with concord of sweet sounds,
Is fit for treasons, stratagems, and spoils.   85

As Portia and Nerissa approach they see the light shining from the house and hear the music. Lorenzo recognises Portia's voice and welcomes her back.

86 **motions of his spirit**: impulses of his mind / inner promptings
   dull: dark / lifeless
87 **affections**: thoughts and feelings
   Erebus: a region of darkness in the classical underworld
88 **Mark**: Listen to
91 **naughty**: wicked

95–6 **his ... itself**: the substitute's dignity drains away
97 **main of waters**: sea

99 **without respect**: until seen or heard in context

101 **bestows ... it**: gives it that special quality

103 **is attended**: 1 listened to; 2 in the company of other birds

THINK ABOUT for GCSE

Language

- What do you think Portia might have in mind when she says 'So shines a good deed in a naughty world' (line 91)?

- Portia says to Nerissa, 'Nothing is good, I see, without respect' (line 99). What examples does Portia give to illustrate that things only have *relative* values, or value in a particular context (lines 92 to 108)?

107 **by season**: by the occasion / at a particular time
   seasoned: made perfect / improved
109 **Endymion**: A young shepherd in Greek mythology, who was made to sleep forever by the moon goddess Diana, who loved him, to preserve his youth and beauty.
110 **would not**: wishes not to be

The motions of his spirit are dull as night,
And his affections dark as Erebus.
Let no such man be trusted. Mark the music.

Enter PORTIA *and* NERISSA, *at a distance.*

PORTIA   That light we see is burning in my hall.
              How far that little candle throws his beams!   **90**
              So shines a good deed in a naughty world.

NERISSA   When the moon shone, we did not see the candle.

PORTIA   So doth the greater glory dim the less.
              A substitute shines brightly as a king
              Until a king be by – and then his state   **95**
              Empties itself, as doth an inland brook
              Into the main of waters. – Music! – Hark!

NERISSA   It is your music, madam, of the house.

PORTIA   Nothing is good, I see, without respect:
              Methinks it sounds much sweeter than by day.   **100**

NERISSA   Silence bestows that virtue on it, madam.

PORTIA   The crow doth sing as sweetly as the lark
              When neither is attended – and I think
              The nightingale, if she should sing by day,
              When every goose is cackling, would be thought   **105**
              No better a musician than the wren.
              How many things by season seasoned are
              To their right praise, and true perfection!
              (*Calling out*) Peace, ho! – The moon sleeps with
                  Endymion,
              And would not be awaked.

The music ceases.

LORENZO   That is the voice,   **110**
              Or I am much deceived, of Portia.

PORTIA   He knows me as the blind man knows the cuckoo –
              By the bad voice.

LORENZO   Dear lady, welcome home!

PORTIA   We have been praying for our husbands' welfare,

Lorenzo reports that Bassanio and Gratiano are expected back soon and Portia orders that no one is to reveal that she has been away. She greets Bassanio when he arrives and then welcomes Antonio.

115 **speed**: prosper

118 **signify**: report

119–20 **take … hence**: make no mention of the fact that we have been away

127 **hold … Antipodes**: experience daylight at the same time as the other side of the world
128 **in … sun**: at night
129 *be* **light**: be sexually promiscuous
130 **heavy**: heavy-hearted

132 **God sort all!**: let it be as God wishes!

THINK ABOUT for GCSE

Language

• What mood is conveyed by Portia's description of the night (lines 124 to 126)?

• What point is Portia making through her play on the word 'light' (lines 129 to 131)? Why might she be deliberately introducing the idea of sexual infidelity here?

135 **bound**: indebted
137 **bound**: 1 tied to Shylock's bond; 2 imprisoned

138 **acquitted of**: freed from

141 **scant**: cut short
this breathing courtesy: these words of politeness

Which speed, we hope, the better for our words. **115**
Are they returned?

LORENZO Madam, they are not yet.
But there is come a messenger before
To signify their coming.

PORTIA Go in, Nerissa.
Give order to my servants that they take
No note at all of our being absent hence – **120**
Nor you, Lorenzo – Jessica, nor you.

A trumpet-call is heard.

LORENZO Your husband is at hand: I hear his trumpet.
We are no tell-tales, madam – fear you not.

PORTIA This night methinks is but the daylight sick –
It looks a little paler – 'tis a day **125**
Such as the day is when the sun is hid.

Enter BASSANIO, ANTONIO *and* GRATIANO, *with their Servants.*

BASSANIO We should hold day with the Antipodes,
If you would walk in absence of the sun.

PORTIA Let me give light, but let me not *be* light,
For a light wife doth make a heavy husband – **130**
And never be Bassanio so for me.
But God sort all! – You are welcome home, my lord.

BASSANIO I thank you, madam. Give welcome to my friend.
This is the man, this is Antonio,
To whom I am so infinitely bound. **135**

PORTIA You should in all sense be much bound to him,
For, as I hear, he was much bound for you.

ANTONIO No more than I am well acquitted of.

PORTIA (*To* ANTONIO) Sir, you are very welcome to our house.
It must appear in other ways than words; **140**
Therefore I scant this breathing courtesy.

GRATIANO (*To* NERISSA) By yonder moon I swear you do me
wrong!
In faith, I gave it to the judge's clerk –

A quarrel breaks out between Nerissa and Gratiano. She accuses him of having given her ring to a woman and refuses to believe his story. Portia takes Nerissa's side, saying that Bassanio would never have parted with the ring she gave him.

THINK ABOUT *for* GCSE

Performance and staging

• What might happen on stage to cause Portia to react with 'A quarrel…!' (line 146)? How might Portia behave during Gratiano's argument with Nerissa (line 147 to 165), given that she already knows what their quarrel is about?

Themes and issues

• **Love and friendship**: What point does Nerissa make about the ring's value, which Gratiano appears not to have understood (lines 147 to 156)?

Performance and staging

• How might Nerissa react to being called 'scrubbèd boy' (line 162)? What might Bassanio do when Portia says 'I gave *my* love a ring…' (line 170)?

144   **Would … gelt**: I wish he were castrated
      for my part: as far as I'm concerned

147   **paltry**: worthless
148   **posy**: message inscribed on a ring
149   **cutler's poetry**: rhymes inscribed on a knife-handle (the equivalent of cheap Christmas-cracker mottoes)

155   **Though**: If
156   **respective**: mindful of its significance

159   **and if**: if

162   **scrubbèd**: stunted / undersized

164   **prating**: talkative / chattering

167   **slightly**: easily

169   **riveted**: bolted / immovably fixed

174   **masters**: possesses
176   **An 'twere to me**: If I had been treated like this

	Would he were gelt that had it for my part,	
	Since you do take it, love, so much at heart.	145
PORTIA	A quarrel, ho – already! What's the matter?	
GRATIANO	About a hoop of gold, a paltry ring	
	That she did give me, whose posy was	
	For all the world like cutler's poetry	
	Upon a knife: 'Love me, and leave me not.'	150
NERISSA	What talk you of the posy or the value?	
	You swore to me when I did give it you	
	That you would wear it till your hour of death,	
	And that it should lie with you in your grave.	
	Though not for me, yet for your vehement oaths	155
	You should have been respective and have kept it.	
	Gave it a judge's clerk! No, God's my judge,	
	The clerk will ne'er wear hair on's face that had it!	
GRATIANO	He will, and if he live to be a man.	
NERISSA	Ay, if a *woman* live to be a man.	160
GRATIANO	Now, by this hand, I gave it to a youth! –	
	A kind of boy, a little scrubbèd boy	
	No higher than thyself, the judge's clerk –	
	A prating boy that begged it as a fee.	
	I could not for my heart deny it him.	165
PORTIA	You were to blame, I must be plain with you,	
	To part so slightly with your wife's first gift,	
	A thing stuck on with oaths upon your finger,	
	And so riveted with faith unto your flesh.	
	I gave *my* love a ring, and made him swear	170
	Never to part with it, and here he stands.	
	I dare be sworn for him he would not leave it	
	Nor pluck it from his finger, for the wealth	
	That the world masters. Now, in faith, Gratiano,	
	You give your wife too unkind a cause of grief.	175
	An 'twere to me, I should be mad at it.	

Gratiano reveals that Bassanio did indeed give his ring away and Portia is angry with him, pointing out how important it was as a symbol of their love. She claims that Nerissa was right – the rings were given to women.

182 **took ... writing**: made (legal) notes
183 **aught**: anything

189 **void**: empty

THINK ABOUT for GCSE

Performance and staging

- What opportunities for comedy are there in lines 179 to 188?

Characterisation

- What do you think Portia is actually feeling during her words with Bassanio about the ring (lines 189 to 208)?

Themes and issues

- **Love and friendship**: What do you think is the significance of the quarrel about the rings at this point in the play?

195 **conceive**: understand
196 **left**: parted with
198 **abate ... displeasure**: not be so angry with me
199 **virtue**: value (as a love-token)
201 **contain**: keep possession of
204 **pleased**: wanted
205 **terms of zeal**: spirited argument
wanted the modesty: would have been so lacking in delicacy / sensitivity
206 **urge**: persist in asking for
held as a ceremony: of such symbolic importance

BASSANIO	(*Aside*) Why, I were best to cut my left hand off,
	And swear I lost the ring defending it.
GRATIANO	My Lord Bassanio gave his ring away
	Unto the judge that begged it, and indeed
	Deserved it too – and then the boy, his clerk,
	That took some pains in writing, he begged mine.
	And neither man nor master would take aught
	But the two rings.
PORTIA	What ring gave you, my lord?
	Not that, I hope, which you received of me.
BASSANIO	If I could add a lie unto a fault,
	I would deny it. But you see my finger
	Hath not the ring upon it: it is gone.
PORTIA	Even so void is your false heart of truth.
	By heaven I will ne'er come in your bed
	Until I see the ring!
NERISSA	(*To* GRATIANO) Nor I in yours
	Till I again see mine!
BASSANIO	Sweet Portia,
	If you did know to whom I gave the ring,
	If you did know *for* whom I gave the ring,
	And would conceive for what I gave the ring,
	And how unwillingly I left the ring,
	When nought would be accepted *but* the ring,
	You would abate the strength of your displeasure.
PORTIA	If you had known the virtue of the ring,
	Or half her worthiness that gave the ring,
	Or your own honour to contain the ring,
	You would not then have parted with the ring.
	What man is there so much unreasonable,
	If you had pleased to have defended it
	With any terms of zeal, wanted the modesty
	To urge the thing held as a ceremony?
	Nerissa teaches me what to believe:
	I'll die for 't, but some woman had the ring!

Line numbers: 180, 185, 190, 195, 200, 205

Bassanio tries in vain to explain why he felt obliged to give the ring to the young lawyer, but Portia and Nerissa both remain angry. They threaten to be unfaithful with the lawyer and his clerk if they ever visit Belmont.

210 **civil doctor**: doctor of civil law

213 **suffered**: caused / let

217 **beset with**: under attack from feelings of **courtesy**: the need to be courteous
219 **besmear it**: spoil it (i.e. my honour)
220 **candles of the night**: stars

THINK ABOUT for GCSE

226 **liberal**: generous

Characterisation

- Antonio has remained silent during the quarrel between Portia and Bassanio. What are his feelings? What might cause him to say 'I am th' unhappy subject of these quarrels' (line 238)?

229 **know**: 1 recognise; 2 have sex with
230 **from**: away from
Argus: A giant in classical mythology, who had one hundred eyes only two of which slept at any one time.
232 **honour**: chastity / chaste reputation
yet mine own: still intact
234 **be well advised**: take care

Performance and staging

- Portia and Antonio have had two exchanges in this scene (lines 138 to 141 and 238 to 239). How might they be performed? Think of reasons why Portia and Antonio might be (a) warm and friendly with one another, or (b) cool and distant. Which interpretation do you prefer?

237 **mar**: spoil
pen: i.e. his penis (pun)

239 **notwithstanding**: despite all this

243 **Mark ... that?**: Just listen to that!

BASSANIO	No, by my honour, madam, by my soul,	
	No woman had it, but a civil doctor,	210

BASSANIO No, by my honour, madam, by my soul,
No woman had it, but a civil doctor,   210
Which did refuse three thousand ducats of me,
And begged the ring – the which I did deny him,
And suffered him to go displeased away,
Even he that had held up the very life
Of my dear friend. What should I say, sweet lady?   215
I was enforced to send it after him;
I was beset with shame and courtesy.
My honour would not let ingratitude
So much besmear it. Pardon me, good lady,
For by these blessèd candles of the night,   220
Had you been there, I think *you* would have begged
The ring of me to give the worthy doctor.

PORTIA Let not that doctor e'er come near my house.
Since he hath got the jewel that I loved,
And that which you did swear to keep for me,   225
I will become as liberal as you.
I'll not deny him anything I have –
No, not my body, nor my husband's bed:
Know him I shall, I am well sure of it.
Lie not a night from home. Watch me like Argus.   230
If you do not, if I be left alone,
Now by mine honour, which is yet mine own,
I'll have that doctor for my bedfellow.

NERISSA – And I his clerk! Therefore be well advised
How you do leave me to mine own protection.   235

GRATIANO Well, do you so! Let not me take him then,
For if I do, I'll mar the young clerk's pen.

ANTONIO I am th' unhappy subject of these quarrels.

PORTIA Sir, grieve not you. You are welcome notwithstanding.

BASSANIO Portia, forgive me this enforcèd wrong,   240
And, in the hearing of these many friends,
I swear to thee, even by thine own fair eyes,
Wherein I see myself –

PORTIA   Mark you but that?
In both my eyes he doubly sees himself –

When Antonio defends his
friend, Portia gives in and
asks Antonio to give Bassanio
another ring. Bassanio is amazed
to find that it is the same ring.
Portia and Nerissa declare that
they were given the rings after
sleeping with the lawyer and
clerk. Portia finally reveals the
truth, and tells Antonio that
three of his ships have returned
safely.

THINK ABOUT for GCSE

Performance and staging

• What are the arguments for
playing this whole 'rings'
sequence (lines 146 to
255) (a) light-heartedly,
for comedy, or (b) to show
that the women take very
seriously the fact that the
men gave their rings away?

Structure and form

• In Act 3, Portia gave control
of herself and her property
to Bassanio. In what ways
do the events here (lines 254
to 277) demonstrate that the
women in one important
sense remain completely in
charge?

245 **by … self**: 1 by the double reflection; 2
as a two-faced deceiver
246 **oath of credit**: believable promise
(ironic)

250 **but for him**: if it were not for the man
251 **Had quite miscarried**: would have been
totally lost / destroyed
252 **My … forfeit**: I pledge my soul (having
once pledged his body)
253 **advisedly**: knowingly
254 **be his surety**: guarantee his truth

258 **of**: from
259 **by**: in exchange for

262 **In lieu of**: in return for

264 **fair enough**: in good enough condition
265 **cuckolds**: men with unfaithful wives
ere: before
266 **grossly**: crudely

272 **even but now**: only a few minutes ago

276 **argosies**: merchant ships
277 **suddenly**: unexpectedly

In each eye one. Swear by your double self –   245
And there's an oath of credit!

BASSANIO   Nay, but hear me.
Pardon this fault, and by my soul I swear
I never more will break an oath with thee.

ANTONIO I once did lend my body for his wealth,
Which, but for him that had your husband's ring,   250
Had quite miscarried. I dare be bound again,
My soul upon the forfeit, that your lord
Will never more break faith advisedly.

PORTIA Then you shall be his surety. Give him this –
And bid him keep it better than the other.   255

She gives a ring to ANTONIO.

ANTONIO Here, Lord Bassanio – swear to keep this ring.

BASSANIO By heaven – it is the same I gave the doctor!

PORTIA I had it of him. Pardon me, Bassanio –
For by this ring the doctor lay with me.

NERISSA – And pardon *me*, my gentle Gratiano –   260
For that same scrubbèd boy, the doctor's clerk,
In lieu of this, (*showing* GRATIANO's *ring*) last night did
   lie with me.

GRATIANO Why – this is like the mending of highways
In summer, where the ways are fair enough!
What, are we cuckolds ere we have deserved it?   265

PORTIA Speak not so grossly. You are all amazed.
Here is a letter – read it at your leisure:
It comes from Padua, from Bellario.
There you shall find that Portia was the doctor,
Nerissa there her clerk. Lorenzo here   270
Shall witness I set forth as soon as you,
And even but now returned. I have not yet
Entered my house. Antonio, you are welcome,
And I have better news in store for you
Than you expect. Unseal this letter soon: 275
There you shall find three of your argosies
Are richly come to harbour suddenly.

In the general amazement, Portia and Nerissa hand Lorenzo a document which assures him and Jessica of all Shylock's wealth when he dies. They all go inside to hear the full story from Portia.

279 chancèd on: came upon by chance
dumb: lost for words

THINK ABOUT for GCSE

Characterisation

- What might Jessica's reaction be to the news that the possessions of 'the rich Jew' will come to her and Lorenzo (lines 291 to 293)?

Performance and staging

- Some productions of this play end cheerfully, with Antonio a rich man again and the three couples celebrating. Others end on a downbeat note, with Antonio still alone and 'sad', Jessica thinking about her father (and still viewed by the Christians as an outsider), and Portia and Nerissa realising that they have married men who may have failed to understand what true love is. How would you direct the ending of the play?

286 living: livelihood

288 road: harbour

292 deed of gift: will (see Act 4, Scene 1, lines 386–8)
293 dies possessed of: possesses when he dies
294 manna: In the Bible, manna was the miraculous food from heaven that sustained the Israelites in the desert.
296–7 you … full: your curiosity will not be satisfied until you know everything that happened
298 charge … inter'gatories: oblige us to answer questions as though we were being examined under oath
301 sworn on: sworn under oath to answer
302 had rather stay: would rather wait

305 couching: in bed
307 So sore: so greatly
ring: (could also mean vagina)

You shall not know by what strange accident
I chancèd on this letter.

ANTONIO   I am dumb!

BASSANIO   Were you the doctor – and I knew you not?   280

GRATIANO   Were you the clerk that is to make me cuckold?

NERISSA   Ay – but the clerk that never means to do it,
Unless he live until he be a man.

BASSANIO   Sweet Doctor, you shall be my bedfellow:
When I am absent, then lie with my wife.   285

ANTONIO   Sweet lady, you have given me life and living –
For here I read for certain that my ships
Are safely come to road.

PORTIA   How now, Lorenzo?
My clerk hath some good comforts too for you.

NERISSA   Ay, and I'll give them him without a fee.   290
There do I give to you and Jessica,
From the rich Jew, a special deed of gift,
After his death, of all he dies possessed of.

LORENZO   Fair ladies, you drop manna in the way
Of starvèd people.

PORTIA   It is almost morning –   295
And yet I am sure you are not satisfied
Of these events at full. Let us go in,
And charge us there upon inter'gatories,
And we will answer all things faithfully.

GRATIANO   Let it be so. The first inter'gatory   300
That my Nerissa shall be sworn on is
Whether till the next night she had rather stay,
Or go to bed now, being two hours to day.
But were the day come, I should wish it dark
Till I were couching with the doctor's clerk.   305
Well – while I live I'll fear no other thing
So sore as keeping safe Nerissa's ring.

All go in together.

JEWS AND ANTI-SEMITISM

Anti-Semitism, the irrational hatred or fear of Jews, has a long and ugly history. By the end of the eleventh century, there were many independent, self-governing Jewish communities throughout Europe, including those in London and other English cities. But Jews were always in a precarious position. The Christian Church taught that they should be hated for their killing of Jesus and believed that they deserved to wander the earth forever. The Church also argued that Jews should not be allowed to employ Christian servants and should be forced to wear distinguishing dress. It was no surprise, therefore, that the population picked up these prejudices and began to spread lies about Jews, claiming that they murdered Christian children during their feast of Passover and used their blood in the baking of unleavened bread. This 'blood libel' was a background to atrocities such as the desperate mass-suicide of Jews in York in 1190, after they had been attacked by a Christian mob, and the many anti-Jewish riots during the twelfth-century Crusades. After a succession of English kings had imposed heavy taxes on Jews in order to increase royal revenues, Edward I finally expelled most Jews from England in 1290, confiscating their lands and possessions.

In the centuries that followed, anti-Jewish hatred spread. During the middle of the fourteenth century, when all Europe was gripped by fear of the Black Death, Jews were accused of poisoning wells, because, as the argument went, the Jews' superior hygiene and diet made them less likely to contract the disease! Even when Jews were largely absent from England (they were re-admitted by Oliver Cromwell in 1656), anti-Jewish stereotypes were being reinforced in the popular imagination through church sermons and religious literature.

Two related questions are therefore often asked about *The Merchant of Venice*. Is it an anti-Semitic play? And, was Shakespeare himself anti-Semitic? There isn't a straightforward answer to either of these questions, but many people argue that it is inappropriate to apply the term 'anti-Semitic' to a play from this period because the anti-Jewish prejudices then were quite different from modern anti-Semitism, both in theory and practice, as they were based on a world view quite different from our own. Some people believe that, whether or not Shakespeare was anti-Semitic, the play as performed today usually is. Their argument is that all the characters who insult Shylock because he is a Jew, or make insulting remarks about Jews in general, are rewarded with wealth or happiness (in some cases both) at the end of the play. They also point out that Shylock's wickedness is associated with Jews in general and that there is no independent voice to speak out against this anti-Jewish speech and behaviour in the play.

JEWS IN SHAKESPEARE'S ENGLAND

It has often been suggested that Shakespeare could not have known any Jews, since they had been expelled from England in 1290 and were not permitted to return until some years after his death. However, there were a small number of Jews in Elizabethan England who had converted to Christianity (mainly from Spain and Portugal) and there is some suggestion that they received visits from other Jews.

One particular Jewish convert had become notorious only three or four years before Shakespeare wrote *The Merchant of Venice*. Ruy Lopez, a physician to Queen Elizabeth, was accused of trying to poison the queen. His trial was notable for the anti-Jewish feeling expressed by everyone present – even the judge called Lopez 'that vile Jew'. Despite the attempts of the Queen herself to postpone his execution, Lopez was hanged in June 1594.

It is impossible to say whether Shakespeare knew any Jews or converts, but *The Merchant of Venice* reflects little in the way of a deep understanding of the Jewish religion and customs beyond the fact that they do not eat pork and worship at a synagogue, facts which were widely known at the time.

JEWS ON STAGE

By the time Shakespeare came to write *The Merchant of Venice*, there had already been influential portrayals of Jews on the English stage. One was Judas, a popular villain in the Mystery plays (dramatisations of Bible stories) that Shakespeare would himself have seen as a child. Performed in a red wig, Judas was represented as the betrayer, the man who accepted '30 pieces of silver' to hand Jesus over to his enemies – and as a Jew.

A more immediate predecessor was *The Jew of Malta* by Shakespeare's great rival, Christopher Marlowe. Written about eight years before *The Merchant of Venice*, Marlowe's powerful and grotesque tragedy featured a memorably villainous Jew in the shape of Barabas, who gloats over his riches, plots people's deaths with Machiavellian delight and dies splendidly in a boiling cauldron.

MONEY-LENDING AND USURY

Throughout the Middle Ages, lending money at interest, known as 'usury', was condemned by the Church. But in 1571, aware that charging interest had become a widespread business practice, a law was passed permitting individuals to charge up to ten per cent interest on loans. Once people had become accustomed to this rate of interest, the term 'usury' came to be applied only to the lending of money at *excessive* rates of interest, and individuals were prosecuted for it. One example was Shakespeare's own father!

By the time Shakespeare came to write *The Merchant of Venice*, therefore, Antonio's opposition to interest might have been surprising to most of the audience. However, although most Christians no longer did business like Antonio, Jews were still condemned for their money-lending, unjustly accused of the exploitation of needy borrowers and the lending of money at a huge profit.

VENICE

By the late thirteenth century, Venice was the most prosperous city in Europe and, although in some decline by Shakespeare's time, remained famous for its wealth, impartial justice, political wisdom and liberal attitudes. Venice was famous for the quality of its justice: unique and strict laws, impartially enforced, gave foreign traders the confidence that they would always be fairly treated.

Many Jews came to Venice, fleeing persecution or even faced with expulsion from their own countries. Unlike most other Christian countries, Venice gave Jews certain legal rights, so long as they paid for them in heavy taxes. In 1516, the Jewish community in Venice was allocated a district called the *ghetto nuovo*. There they could build their own places of worship and employ their own butchers and bakers to prepare food according to Jewish customs. The colony quickly grew and its name has given us our modern word 'ghetto'.

Venetian Jews enjoyed much more freedom than their counterparts anywhere else in Europe. They were allowed to trade, they were protected from physical violence by law and there were many examples of friendly relations between Jews and Christians. On the other hand, Jews in Venice were not allowed to own property and had to be locked into the fortress-like ghetto every night and on Christian holidays. Every Jew was also required to wear a yellow hat or turban (later changed to red). Many of these restrictions, however, were lifted during Shakespeare's lifetime and there is no doubt that Venice benefited greatly from its Jewish population, who brought a great deal of trade to the city.

This was part of the context in which Shakespeare came to write *The Merchant of Venice*. We cannot know to what extent he was influenced by the earlier presentations of stage Jews, notably in the persons of Judas and Marlowe's Barabas, but it is safe to assume that, as a businessman, he knew all about money-lending and had a close familiarity with the Bible. The modern context to this play is, of course, different, living as we still do under the shadow of the Holocaust. When modern actors and directors perform *The Merchant of Venice*, they are keenly aware that many people find the play deeply offensive, and they usually strive to avoid anything that might be viewed as an anti-Semitic interpretation.

THEATRE AND STAGE
The Merchant of Venice probably dates from 1596–97. Its first performances by Shakespeare's acting company (then known as the Lord Chamberlain's Men) probably took place in the playhouse simply called 'The Theatre', in Shoreditch, on what was then the north-east edge of London. This playhouse was of the same familiar type as the more famous Globe. The Theatre, in fact, was pulled down in 1598 and its timbers re-used for building the Globe – so the size of the stage, with the yard and galleries round it, was probably much the same.

What we know about the early staging of *The Merchant of Venice* comes mainly from the evidence of its text and stage directions. Most important is the continuous and varying use of the large main-stage platform on which most of the action of the play takes place. Only one scene, Act 2 Scene 6, has action on a level above the main stage, when Jessica appears '*above*', at her window, before she runs away with Lorenzo.

Position on the wide main-stage was very important. Formal or ceremonial scenes would tend to be performed from the back of the stage – where the Duke of Venice might preside over the trial scene in *The Merchant of Venice*, or where the three caskets might appear. Less formal scenes would be played out on the open fore-stage, surrounded by the standing audience in the unroofed theatre-yard. Scenes where characters speak 'aside' to the audience, as when Shylock meets Antonio in Act 1 Scene 3 ('How like a fawning publican he looks!'), would require a relatively close contact with the audience.

ACTION AND SETTINGS
The action of *The Merchant of Venice* in an Elizabethan theatre would have been fast and continuous, with no intervals between Acts or Scenes. New scenes are often marked simply by the entrance of new characters. When Portia and Nerissa appear for Act 1 Scene 2, it is clear that action has moved from Venice to Belmont. The only clue an early audience would have needed to imagine this transition is Bassanio's talk of 'Belmont' and 'fair Portia', as he seeks to borrow money from Antonio. No scenery or stage lighting, as we think of them, was used. The play's language and activity were enough to suggest places and settings to the imagination of its audience.

In this theatre, buildings for indoor and outdoor scenes were represented only by the rising wall behind the stage, with its raised gallery (about three metres above the stage) and two main doors. Jessica comes down from this gallery to re-enter below and elope with Lorenzo (Act 2 Scene 6), but it would otherwise have been used only by the musicians of the company. Gratiano, Salerio, and Lorenzo meet for the elopement scene under a 'penthouse' – a word used for the overhang of a building, but which may also have referred to the canopy over the stage of the Theatre (held up by its two great columns). The rear-stage wall here represents the outside of Shylock's house, but it could just as easily represent 'buildings of Venice' or an interior wall for 'indoor' scenes – inside Portia's Belmont or inside the law-court for the great trial scene (Act 4 Scene 1). In Act 5, it will represent Belmont as seen from its gardens, to which Portia and Bassanio return.

Between the stage doors of the Theatre (as at the Globe) would have been a third central opening, usually curtained off. This was known as the 'discovery' space, because special props (such as beds or tombs) could be pushed out from it or revealed ('discovered') inside it. This recess was probably used for the three 'casket' scenes (Act 2 Scenes 7 and 9, and Act 3 Scene 2). The three caskets were evidently revealed by drawing curtains apart, and they may even have been on a decorated framework pushed forward onto the stage.

Even without scenery, the stage of the Theatre would not necessarily have been bare. Stagehands might have brought out props to assist some scenes, such as seats for indoor scenes and a throne for the Duke in the trial scene. The property list of another Elizabethan acting company included items like 'moss banks', which would have been used for a garden scene – as when Lorenzo and Jessica listen to the music of Belmont in Act 5 Scene 1 ('How sweet the moonlight sleeps upon this bank! Here will we sit…').

Night-time scenes in the real daylight of an open Elizabethan theatre were suggested by actors carrying burning torches or candles. In Act 2 Scene 6, Jessica is to be Lorenzo's 'torch-bearer' for the masque that night. In Act 5, it is the language of the play that creates the night – with Lorenzo and Jessica's echoing 'In such a night as this…' and by constant references to moonlight. When Lorenzo describes the stars over Belmont ('Look how the floor of heaven is thick inlaid with patens [spangles] of bright gold'), he may well have gestured up to the canopy over the stage (known as 'the heavens'), the underside of which may have been painted with stars and the zodiac, as it was at the Globe.

To complete the romantic atmosphere, Portia's 'music' (musicians who normally played from the gallery) enters to provide soft accompanying 'night-music'. When Portia and Bassanio come home to Belmont, their servants would probably have carried lights. Lancelot Gobbo, typically, has entered pretending he can't find Lorenzo in the 'darkness' of the 'garden'. Portia sees a 'little candle' shining from her house, and suggests that the night is becoming lighter ('as the day is when the sun is hid').

This final 'night-time back at Belmont' scene of the play is unusual because it suggests that Portia and Nerissa, if not Bassanio and Antonio and their servants, may even have entered through the audience in the theatre-yard. The stage is Belmont's 'garden' (with the 'house' behind it), and there is a strong sense of approach from a distance. Entry through the audience was rare in Shakespeare's theatre, but this last scene of arrival and reunion at Belmont may have been an example.

COSTUMES AND DISGUISES

Costumes were the most valuable possessions of Elizabethan theatre companies (often worth far more than the sums paid for plays) and they served as strong signs of rank, wealth and character. In *The Merchant of Venice*, there would have been a clear contrast between the luxurious dress of Portia (a vastly wealthy heiress) and that of Nerissa (her waiting-woman or maid). Before Bassanio borrows money to be Portia's suitor, he would have been more 'poorly' dressed than the 'wealthy' Bassanio who arrives at Belmont. Servants would have been dressed in the liveries (uniform and badge) of their employers. Bassanio is seen ordering clothes for his new servants in Act 2 Scene 2: Lancelot Gobbo is given 'a livery more guarded' (with more braid or decoration) than his fellow-servants, although this may also suggest a jester's costume.

Some characters would have been marked out as 'different' by costume – a major theme of the comedy. Antonio's costume may have been darker than Bassanio's or Gratiano's (to go with his melancholy). Shylock would have worn his 'Jewish gaberdine' (Act 1 Scene 3), the dark robe marking his 'alien' status in Venice. We know little about how he might have been made up. Suggestions that he was played with red hair, or with an exaggerated nose (a racist stereotype), have more to do with an older tradition – of how the hated character of Judas was presented in medieval religious drama.

Female parts in Shakespeare's theatre were played by male actors, almost always by the highly trained 'apprentice' boys of the company. Audiences were used to expert female impersonation: Portia, Nerissa, and Jessica would all have been played by boys. Disguise was another familiar convention of Elizabethan drama – almost always impossible for other characters in a play to see through, unless they (like the audience) already know the secret. Portia and Nerissa are therefore 'unrecognisable', in the trial scene (Act 4 Scene 1), in their disguises as 'Balthazar' and his clerk.

Shakespeare was writing for performers he knew well: Lancelot Gobbo, for instance, was a part for his company's famous comedian, Will Kemp. The scene in which Lancelot plays tricks on his blind father is a classic Elizabethan 'clown routine' (audiences of Shakespeare's day being more relaxed about laughing at disability than we might be today).

The Merchant of Venice remains one of Shakespeare's most popular comedies, even though its presentations of prejudice are sometimes disturbing. Its staging in the Elizabethan theatre may seem simple by modern standards, but it was extremely effective in playing to the imaginations and emotions of its audiences.

A play in performance at the reconstruction of Shakespeare's Globe

Because some of its content is anti-Semitic, *The Merchant of Venice* is a challenging play to study and to perform. Christian characters taunt Shylock for his religion, calling him a dog, a wolf and a devil, and use the word 'Jew' as a term of abuse. Antonio brazenly admits to spitting on Shylock and promises him he will do so again. At no time in the play is this anti-Semitic behaviour ever criticised – except by Shylock himself. In fact, all the anti-Semites are rewarded by the end of the play either with promotion (Lancelot Gobbo), renewed wealth (Antonio), sudden unearned wealth (Lorenzo) or a productive marriage (Bassanio and Gratiano). Shylock himself is punished under a law that applies especially to 'aliens'.

Shylock's wickedness (he does, after all, plot to cut flesh from a man in cold blood) is also linked by several characters to his being a Jew. If we are to believe Antonio's allegations in court, all Jews are cruel and merciless, and no Christian in the play ever disputes that.

How can a production of *The Merchant of Venice* avoid giving the impression that Jews deserve to be insulted and oppressed, or that anti-Semitism is an acceptable mode of behaviour to be not just tolerated, but rewarded?

SHYLOCK AND ANTI-SEMITISM
Some productions have portrayed Shylock not as a villain, but as a victim worthy of our sympathy. To do so, directors have found ways to soften Shylock's murderous intentions and the hatred that drives him to demand the pound of flesh.

In the late nineteenth century, Sir Henry Irving portrayed Shylock as a tragic hero and ended the trial scene with Shylock staggering, a broken man, from the courtroom. When Sir Laurence Olivier played Shylock in 1970 (directed by **Jonathan Miller** for the National Theatre), he offered the bond sincerely, in an attempt to join the Christian community that was excluding him. Olivier's Shylock turned the bond into a weapon against Antonio only when Jessica had betrayed him by running away with a Christian. In a 2007 production (directed by **Darko Tresnjak**) that ran in New York and Stratford-upon-Avon, the actor playing Shylock took the opposite approach, making him as hard and tough as possible. He had discovered that by *not* striving to win the audience over, they felt more, not less, sympathy for Shylock in the end.

There have been several productions that have set the story in the 1930s, a time when anti-Semitism was growing throughout much of Europe, including Venice. This was the setting for the 1999 National Theatre production (directed by **Trevor Nunn**) in which Henry Goodman's Shylock was a good-natured and devout Jew, tired of the old hatred between himself and Antonio, who offered the bond in a genuine act of friendship. To make this interpretation work, however, the director cut part or all of Shylock's key aside when he first sees Antonio in Act 1 Scene 3, lines 36 to 47. Without that speech, in which Shylock tells us that he hates Antonio and will 'feed fat' his revenge if he gets the chance, actors are able to remove all his initial murderous intent and give the impression that he resolves to kill Antonio only when he is deranged by the loss of his daughter. Cutting the aside works dramatically, but it leaves us with a Shylock of the director's creation, not Shakespeare's.

Setting a production in Shakespeare's own time with the rationale that this is simply how people thought in this period can solve some difficulties. However, it is an unsettling experience to hear Shylock hissed by the audience, as happened in the Globe production of 1998, and risks reinforcing an anti-Semitic stereotype. The 2004 film, starring Al Pacino and directed by **Michael Radford**, also set the play in the sixteenth century. A long prologue showed Jews being attacked by a howling Christian mob and captions explained the context of anti-Semitism and the origin of the word 'ghetto'. The anti-Semites still came out on top, however, and the last sight of Shylock was as a man excluded by the Jewish community.

Venice and Belmont
There has also been a recent move to expose the play's anti-Semitism and highlight the Christians' less admirable qualities, portraying them as both money-obsessed and deeply prejudiced. In the Royal Shakespeare Company production of 1993 (directed by **David Thacker**), Venice was a replica of the City of London, with glass-sided office blocks, computers and mobile phones. When Shylock warned his daughter against looking out of the window at the Christian revellers, the audience sympathised with him – Lorenzo's 'masque' was played as a sex- and alcohol-fuelled office party that any caring parent would hate.

Darko Tresnjak's production used a similar setting, America's business centre, Wall Street, with Belmont as a high-tech as Venice and the suitors choosing between three differently-coloured laptops.

Lorenzo's Act 5 description of the pastoral beauties of Belmont can make a strong contrast with the hard commercialism of Venice, but given the marriage marketing that both Portia and Nerissa engage in, the two places seem more alike than not in most modern productions. **Michael Radford**'s 2004 film contrasts the real with the imaginary in the two locations; he capitalises on the beauties of Venice in his location shots, but relies on sumptuous but rather anonymous interiors to depict Belmont's fairytale palace. The architecture of Venice almost becomes another character in the film, as the director invites the audience to think of the characters as historical people living in sixteenth-century Italy; but he does not clarify the character of Portia's home.

ENDING

Although *The Merchant of Venice* is listed among Shakespeare's comedies, modern audiences tend to view it as a more serious play and productions often end ambiguously, with characters excluded or unhappy.

Shylock, of course, disappears from the play script in Act 4, but he is referred to several times at the end of the play and is never allowed to be far from the audience's minds, or from the thoughts of the characters. The ending of the **Michael Radford** film shows us the ghetto doors being shut on Shylock, and Jessica, still in Belmont, is staring miserably out to sea. In **Jonathan Miller**'s National Theatre production, Jessica was left outside the house, never having been truly welcomed by the Christians and we heard a violin play a Jewish hymn of mourning.

Two recent interpretations have tried to show that although the Christians profit financially at the end, they are far from happy. **Trevor Nunn**'s National Theatre production ended with a Portia speech taken from earlier in Act 5: 'The light methinks is but the daylight sick…' (Act 5 Scene 1, lines 124 to 126) and the characters froze, making no reply.

The **Darko Tresnjak** production had an even more sombre ending. As Act 5 progressed and the men tried in vain to laugh off their giving away of the rings, it clearly dawned on Portia and Nerissa that Bassanio and Gratiano were worthless. The final straw was Gratiano's obscene pun about Nerissa (Act 5 Scene 1, line 307). The women sighed heavily, turned their backs on the men, and the lights dimmed.

ASSESSMENT OF SHAKESPEARE IN YOUR ENGLISH LITERATURE GCSE

All students studying GCSE English Literature have to study at least six texts, three of which are from the English, Welsh or Irish literary heritage. These texts must include prose, poetry and drama, and in England this must include a play by Shakespeare.

The four major exam boards: AQA, Edexcel, WJEC and OCR, include Shakespeare as part of their specifications for English Literature. All the exam boards offer controlled assessment to assess their students' understanding of Shakespeare, although some offer a traditional examination as an alternative option, or as one element of the assessment.

This section of the book offers guidance and support to help you prepare for your GCSE assessment on Shakespeare. The first part (pages 202–4) is relevant to all students, whichever exam board's course you are taking. The second part (pages 205–21) is board-specific, and you should turn to those pages that are relevant to your exam board. Your teacher will advise you if you are unsure which board you are working with.

WHAT YOU WILL BE ASSESSED ON

In your English Literature GCSE you will be marked on various Assessment Objectives (AOs). These assess your ability to:

- **AO1: respond to texts critically and imaginatively; select and evaluate relevant textual detail to illustrate and support interpretations**
  This means that you should show insight and imagination when writing about the text, showing understanding of what the author is saying and how he or she is saying it; and use quotations or direct references to the text to support your ideas and point of view.

- **AO2: explain how language, structure and form contribute to writers' presentation of ideas, themes and settings**
  This means that you need to explain how writers use language (vocabulary, imagery and other literary features), structure and form (the 'shape' of the text) to present ideas, themes and settings (where the action takes place).

- **AO3: make comparisons and explain links between texts, evaluating writers' different ways of expressing meaning and achieving effects**
  This means that you need to compare and link texts, identifying what they have in common and looking at how different writers express meaning and create specific effects for the reader/audience.

- **AO4: relate texts to their social, cultural and historical contexts; explain how texts have been influential and significant to self and other readers in different contexts and at different times**
  This means that, where it is relevant, you need to show awareness of the social, cultural and historical background of the texts; explain the influence of texts on yourself and other readers in different places and times.

You will also be assessed on the **Quality of your Written Communication**. This means you need to ensure that: your text is legible and your spelling, punctuation and grammar are accurate so that the meaning is clear; you choose a style of writing that is suitable for the task; you organise information clearly and logically, using specialist words where relevant.

Not all exam boards assess all the AOs as part of the English Literature Shakespeare task. Here is a summary:

Exam Board	Unit	AO1	AO2	AO3	AO4
AQA	Unit 3 CA	✓	✓	✓	✓
Edexcel	Unit 3 CA		✓	✓	
WJEC	Unit 3 CA	✓	✓	✓	
OCR	Unit 1 CA	✓			

WHAT IS CONTROLLED ASSESSMENT?

Controlled assessment is a way of testing students' knowledge and ability. It differs from an examination in that you will be given the task in advance so you can research and prepare for it, before sitting down to write a full response to it under supervised conditions.

Exam boards differ in the detail of their controlled assessment rules, so do check them out in the board-specific section. However, the general stages of controlled assessment are as follows:

1. **The task**
   Every year exam boards either set a specific task or offer a choice. Your teacher might adapt one of the tasks to suit you and the resources available. You will be given this task well in advance of having to respond to it, so you have plenty of time to prepare for it.

2. Planning and research

Your teacher will have helped you study your text and taught you how to approach the topics. He or she will now advise you on how to carry out further research and plan for your task.

- During this phase you can work with others, for example discussing ideas and sharing resources on the internet.

- Your teacher can give you general feedback during this phase, but not detailed advice.

- You must keep a record of all the source materials you use, including websites.

3. Writing up the response

This will take place under timed, supervised conditions.

- It may be split into more than one session, in which case your teacher will collect your work at the end of the session and put it away until the beginning of the next. You will not have access to it between sessions.

- You may be allowed to take an **un-annotated copy** of the text into the session.

- You may be allowed to take in some brief **notes**.

- You may be allowed access to a **dictionary** or a **thesaurus.**

- You may be allowed to produce your assessment on a computer, but you will not be allowed access to the internet, email, disks or memory sticks.

- During this time, you may not communicate with other candidates. The work you produce must be entirely **your own**.

- Your teacher will advise you on how much you should aim to write.

4. Marking

Your Controlled Assessment Task will be marked by your teacher and may be moderated (supervised and checked) by your exam board.

General examiners' note

Remember:

- you will get marks for responding to the task, but not for writing other material that is not relevant

- you must produce an **individual** response to the task in the final assessment, even if you have discussed ideas with other students previously.

How to succeed in AQA English Literature

If you are studying *The Merchant of Venice* for AQA your knowledge and understanding of the play will be tested in a Controlled Assessment Task. In this task you will have to write about *The Merchant of Venice* and one other text that your teacher will choose. This other text may be a novel, a selection of poetry, another play or even another Shakespeare play. The two texts will be linked in some way and you need to write about both in detail.

Examiner's tip
You will be assessed on the following objectives when responding to your Shakespeare task: AO1, AO2, AO3, AO4. Refer back to pages 202–3 for more about these assessment objectives.

The task

AQA will give your teacher a number of tasks to choose from. There are two main topics:

1. **Themes and ideas**
   This might mean writing about love or loyalty, revenge or forgiveness, racism or sexism or prejudice. For example: *Explore the ways writers present and use the ideas of justice and fairness in the texts you have studied*, **or** *Explore the ways writers have presented conflict in the texts you have studied.*

2. **Characterisation and voice**
   This might mean writing about relationships, young and old characters, or characters from different backgrounds. For example: *Explore the ways texts show differences between men and women* **or** *Explore the ways in which villains are presented in texts you have studied.*

Your response

- You have to complete a written response to ONE task. This should be about 2,000 words, but remember that it's quality not quantity that counts.

- You have FOUR hours to produce your work. Your teacher will probably ask you to complete the task over separate sessions rather than in a single sitting.

- Your teacher will give you plenty of time to prepare for the task. You can use any resources you like, but do keep a record of them (including websites). You must include a list of these at the end of your task.

- You can work in a small group to research and prepare your material but your final work must be all your own.

- Do watch different versions of the play. You can refer to the different versions when you write your response and you will be given credit for this.
- You can refer to brief notes when you are writing your response, but these must be brief. You must hand in your notes at the end of each session and on completion of the task. You can also use a copy of the play without any annotations.
- You can handwrite your response or use a word processor. You are allowed a dictionary and thesaurus or grammar and spell-check programs. You are NOT allowed to use the internet, email, disks or memory sticks when writing your response.
- You can do the Controlled Assessment Task in January or June. When you have finished, your teachers will mark your work and then send a sample from your school to AQA to be checked.

Examiner's tip
The Controlled Assessment Task is worth 25 per cent of your final English Literature mark – so it's worth doing it well.

How to get a good grade

1. Select what you write about carefully. It is better to write a lot about a little. Concentrate on one scene in Shakespeare and one chapter in a novel or a single poem, or on two characters, one from a Shakespeare play and one from a novel.
2. Use short, relevant quotations. Every time you include a quotation, consider the language the writer has used and the probable effect on the audience.
3. Never retell the story. You and your teachers already know it. If you find yourself doing this, stop and refocus on the question.
4. Check your spellings, in particular writers' and characters' names.
5. Always remember that Antonio, Shylock, Portia and all the other characters in the play are not real. Do not write about them as if they are. They have been created by Shakespeare: his play is the important thing to consider.

> Explore the ways writers present differences between men and women.

Here and on the next page are extracts from responses written by two students. Both are writing about the meeting between Portia and Bassanio in Act 3 Scene 2.

Extract 1 – Grade C response

Relevant textual detail

Clear explanation

Awareness of effect on audience

Relevant textual detail

Could be developed more

In this scene, Portia tells Bassanio that she wishes she was much more fair and much more rich so that she would be a better wife. She then says that she is very young and innocent and calls herself 'an unlessoned girl, unschooled, unpractised'. The triplet moves from lesson to school to behaviour and tells the audience that she thinks she still has a great deal to learn. Perhaps she is trying to exaggerate her innocence to make her seem more attractive. She also says that she is capable of learning how to be a good wife and that Bassanio is now 'her lord, her governor, her king'. These three roles gradually rise in importance until she says Bassanio will be her king, which means she will be his subject. She has suddenly gone from being a rich young girl in charge of her own fortune and servants to being his subject. She must love him a lot.

Examiner's comments

- The ideas here are expressed clearly and appropriately.
- The student has a good understanding of the text and demonstrates how Shakespeare has used a linguistic device (the triplets) twice in the speech. These examples are sensibly explained and there is evidence of a personal response in the comment that Portia might be trying to make herself appear more attractive.
- The student also explains what Bassanio's choice means to Portia: her lost autonomy.
- The final comment, though a personal response, is undeveloped.
- To raise the grade, the student needs to develop ideas in more detail, including more consideration of Shakespeare's use of language, and to consider more closely the possible effects this speech would have on an audience.
- As it stands, this is a Grade C response.

Extract 2 – Grade A response

The correct casket chosen, Portia draws up an inventory of 'the full sum of me'. In a play dominated by money and, to a lesser extent, value, she tells Bassanio that, 'This house, these servants, and this same myself / Are yours – my lord's'. The final word is important: whilst she is directly addressing Bassanio she is also using the genitive to indicate possession – she, and everything she had until a few moments ago, now belong to someone else. In this world of argosies, usury and debt collection, Portia herself has become little more than a commodity, a man's possession. This change is emphasised by the seeming confusion of the preceding lines. Portia says that she 'was the lord / Of this fair mansion, master of my servants, Queen o'er myself'. Shakespeare gives her two masculine roles as self-descriptions but she finishes with a feminine role. Perhaps, through Portia, he is implying that to be in charge of land and servants is an essentially masculine activity. Certainly, whilst she wishes she were 'A thousand times more fair' she also wishes she were 'ten thousand times more rich', equating personal value with the size of one's bank account.

> Clear use of detail

> Analysis linked to theme

> Detailed analysis

> Sophisticated insight into theme

Examiner's comments

- The ideas are expressed cogently and persuasively and text references are apt.
- There is evidence of imagination in the development of the interpretation and there is a confident exploration of lines, phrases and even individual words, for example the difference between 'my lord' and 'my lord's'.
- The student has written a lot about a little but has also managed to link this to a consideration of the ideas which can be found in the whole text, exploring some of the play's themes and showing awareness that Portia is Shakespeare's dramatic construct.
- This is an example of a Grade A response.

How to succeed in Edexcel English Literature

The response to Shakespeare in Edexcel GCSE English Literature is a Controlled Assessment Task. You must produce your work at school or college under supervision and within two hours, although you may do some preparation for it in advance.

The task

The task will ask you to compare and make links between your own reading of the Shakespeare text and an adaptation. The adaptation can be a film, TV production, musical, graphic novel, audio version or a cartoon, but all must be based on the original play. The task will focus on **one** of the following aspects of the play:

- **Characterisation**
  For example, a study of the importance and development of one of the main characters in the play.

- **Stagecraft**
  For example, looking at ways in which the decisions taken about the staging and set influence the production.

- **Theme**
  For example, the importance of justice and revenge in the play.

- **Relationships**
  For example, the relationship between Antonio and Bassanio, or Jessica and Lorenzo.

Note that your answer should include some discussion of dramatic devices. These include a range of theatrical techniques and styles used by the playwright to create a particular effect on the audience, such as soliloquies, monologues; juxtaposition and contrast; use of dramatic irony; use of the stage and props; actions and reactions.

Preparing your response

When preparing, you will be able to use a range of resources available at your centre, such as the internet, TV, videos and film, live performances, and notes made in class.

You must complete your task individually, without intervention or assistance from others. However, you will be able to use:

- copies of the text without any annotations written in them
- notes (bullet or numbered points, but not a prepared draft or continuous phrases/sentences or paragraphs)
- a dictionary or thesaurus
- grammar or spell-check programs.

How to get a good grade

To get a good mark in this response, it is important that you:

- respond to the chosen drama text critically and imaginatively
- make comparisons and explain links with your own reading
- look at different ways that a production or adaptation expresses ideas
- consider what Shakespeare means and how he achieves his effects
- support your ideas by including evidence from the words of the play.

Activities

The following approaches will help you to explore *The Merchant of Venice* in preparation for the controlled assessment.

Activity 1: Characterisation

Draw up a page with two columns, one for each of two characters. List key headings under which to note down your ideas about each character, for example: personality and temperament; what motivates the character; how the character speaks to other characters. Include supporting references. Do the same for the chosen characters in the adaptation.

Activity 2: Stagecraft

In a group, plan a performance/adaptation of the play. Give each member of the group a non-acting role in the production, such as producer, costume and make-up, props, lighting, sound, or set design. Decide on the most important decisions or tasks which each member has to undertake and make notes on each.

Activity 3: Theme

As you study *The Merchant of Venice*, decide on **two** important themes (e.g. love and revenge), and note down moments in the play that deal with these. Give brief supporting references from the text.

Activity 4: Relationships

Divide a page into three columns, with the headings 'Lorenzo', 'Jessica' and 'their relationship'. Note down your key ideas, for example: Jessica – position in her father's house; self-esteem; the place of religion; Lorenzo – strengths/weaknesses in his character; his interest in money; attitudes to Jessica; their relationship – why they are attracted; difficulties they face. Develop your ideas and support them with brief references.

SAMPLE CONTROLLED ASSESSMENT TASK

> - Choose one key theme in the Shakespeare drama text you have studied. Compare your reading of the theme with the presentation of the same theme in an adaptation.
> - Use examples from the text in your response.

Here are extracts from essays by two candidates who both watched the 2004 film version of *The Merchant of Venice* and compared this with their own reading of the play.

Extract 1 – Grade C response

The theme of race and religion, especially anti-Jewishness is very important in the play. There are huge differences between the Christians and the Jews. The Christian characters prefer human relationships to business, but Shylock is only interested in making and keeping money (or so the Christians think). Antonio lends money free to Bassanio but when Jessica elopes, Shylock runs through the streets crying, 'O, my ducats! O, my daughter!' He thinks money is as important as his daughter. Because Shylock seems so angry and is described by the other characters as 'a devil', or 'A goodly apple rotten at the heart', and because we know he is Jewish, you could think that Shakespeare hated Jewish people. Either way, Shylock hates the others just as much: 'I hate him for he is a Christian'. It is not just one-sided otherwise you could accuse Shakespeare of being racist.

It seems normal to the characters to hate Jews. That can be a shock to people now. But in the Middle Ages, Jews were thrown out of England and it would have been all right to hate them even if it is wrong to us now. This makes the film of the play interesting, as Al Pacino plays Shylock as more sympathetic. He is angry and has weaknesses but that makes him real. He has been spat on and insulted so you understand why he is vicious and hateful, even if it is not right. In the end though, it is Shakespeare's original words which show that he thinks Jews are no worse than Christians: 'If you prick us, do we not bleed?'

Marginal annotations:

- Sound statement but expression could be stronger
- [a]pt quotation [an]d comments [su]pport it
- Sweeping statement, needs justification
- Awareness of context
- [F]air point, [b]ut better [t]o refer to [fi]lm earlier
- Personal viewpoint

Examiner's comments

- The candidate is beginning to make some appropriate comparative points about the film.
- Quotations are appropriate, but do not always fully support the points made.
- Some statements are sweeping and need more justification.
- Personal viewpoints are given but the moral issues could be explored in a more critical way.
- To raise the grade, the answer needs to increase the level of analysis and show a more personal interpretation of the themes.
- As it stands, this is a Grade C response.

Extract 2 – Grade A response

It is, in my opinion, a fallacy that <u>The Merchant of Venice</u> should be described as an anti-Semitic play, critical of the Jewish race and religion. This simplistic view is indeed challenged strongly by the 2004 film version, with Al Pacino as Shylock. Religion and race are crucial to an interpretation of the play. At the time the play was written, it was accepted for English people to despise Jewish people (who were actually expelled from England). In Shakespeare's day, Jews were often portrayed as ugly and avaricious, like the insulting caricature in Marlowe's <u>The Jew of Malta</u>, a play that certainly influenced Shakespeare. However, if you look closely at Shakespeare's text, bigotry and hatred on account of religion are seen to be universal, not reserved for Shylock. Antonio had spat on Shylock and mistreated him because he is Jewish, but similarly, Shylock has said of him: 'I hate him for he is a Christian.' Shakespeare shows that violence and religious hatred only lead to more reactive behaviour: 'The villainy you teach me I will execute – and it shall go hard but I will better the instruction'. This is a theme which is particularly resonant in modern society.

The film picks up on these ideas. The words Shakespeare has written show that Christians can behave as badly or as well as the Jews and vice versa. The way that Al Pacino plays the character of Shylock gives him more dimensions and complexity than a straightforward stereotypical villain. He is angry, but can also speak with a quiet dignity and we are shown the motivations for his anger through the religious bigotry he has suffered. We may not agree with his actions, but we can sympathise with his humiliation and anger in a powerful soliloquy that puts to rest any niggling doubts that Shakespeare was anti-Semitic himself, and shows he is interested in common humanity: 'Hath not a Jew eyes? ... If you poison us, do we not die?'

Side annotations:

Good early reference to the film

Appropriate cross-reference shows knowledge

Confident language, shows contemporary relevance of theme

Thoughtful insight to Shylock's attitudes and behaviour

Evidence of sensitive ability to interpret character

Well-observed – a powerful case for fair treatment of all races

Examiner's comments

- The candidate shows the ability to offer clear, discriminating explanations and interpretations.
- Examples have been chosen very well, and the study of the modern film has enriched the candidate's understanding of the text.
- The writing is fluent, assured and perceptive.
- This is a Grade A response.

How to succeed in WJEC English Literature

If you are entered for GSCE English Literature (or GCSE English) you will be assessed on Shakespeare in a Controlled Assessment Task. This task will be a linked assignment, which means you need to write about the Shakespeare play you have studied, in this case, *The Merchant of Venice*, and some poetry you have studied in class. The play and poems will be linked by a theme. The possible themes are:

* love
* family and parent/child relationships
* youth/age
* power and ambition
* male/female relationships/role of women
* hypocrisy/prejudice
* conflict
* grief.

WJEC, the examination board, will specify which themes are set for the year you take the exam, and your teacher will decide which theme to focus on, according to the Shakespeare play and the poems you have studied.

The task

The examination board will provide teachers with 'generic tasks'. These are general tasks that your teacher will modify to suit the class and the texts you are studying. For example, the generic task could be:

Many plays and poems are about prejudice. Consider the presentation of prejudice in a Shakespeare play and link it with poetry which also deals with the theme of prejudice.

Your teacher will modify the task and may break it down into three sections, such as:

Look at the way Shakespeare presents prejudice in the trial scene, Act 4 Scene 1, of *The Merchant of Venice*.

Consider the way prejudice is presented in some of the poems in the collection. Choose one poem to write about in particular, but make references to others.

What is your personal response to the literature you have studied? In your answer, explore links between the poetry and *The Merchant of Venice*.

Activity

Think about how you would approach the task above, and write a plan for your response to the first part of the task.

You might want to:

- make notes on the main events of the scene, particularly parts where prejudice is evident. You'll also need to briefly put the scene in context: what has led up to these events?
- underline, or make a note of, key words and phrases and explain how they are effective.

PREPARING YOUR RESPONSE

- You will have up to fifteen hours to prepare your response, then up to four hours to write it up.
- While you are doing your research and planning, you will have limited supervision; you may use research materials, you can work with others in your class, and your teachers will be able to give you general advice.
- Any worksheets your teacher provides to help you will be sent to the external moderator, and your teacher will have to tell the examination board about the support you have had.
- You are allowed to take an A4 sheet of notes into the final assessment. This will be checked, by an external moderator, to see that it is not a draft or detailed plan.

WRITING YOUR RESPONSE

- Once you start writing, you will be formally supervised (a bit like in an exam).
- You may complete the assignment over several sessions, in which case, your teacher will collect the work in at the end of each session.
- You are not allowed to discuss your work with others (other students or teachers) during this part of the assessment.
- You will be allowed to use a dictionary or thesaurus if you need to, and you may be allowed to produce the work on a word processor.
- The approximate length for this assignment is 2,000 words but quality is more important than quantity.

HOW TO GET A GOOD GRADE

Be prepared to discuss characters and relationships sensitively in both the Shakespeare play and the poetry. You will be expected to show detailed knowledge of both, through well chosen, brief quotations and direct reference to the texts, in order to back up the points you make.

You need to aim to show your understanding of how the texts are written, by exploring, for example, the use of language and its effects. Do not try to simply identify literary features, for instance writing 'There are several metaphors used' or something similar. These features are only of interest if you explain why and how they are used and the effects they create.

Do explain the links and connections between the texts carefully.

- Look at the way Shakespeare presents Jessica's relationship with her father, Shylock, in *The Merchant of Venice*.
- Consider the way some of the poets in the collection present relationships between parents and children. Write about the way the relationship between a parent and child is presented in one poem in particular, but make reference to others.
- What is your personal response to the literature you have studied here? In your answer, explore the links between the poetry and *The Merchant of Venice*.

Here and on the following page are extracts from essays by two students, answering the first part of the task.

Extract 1 – Grade C response

Some focus and context

Shylock is the Jewish money-lender in The Merchant of Venice. At the beginning of the play he lives with his daughter, Jessica, and their servant Lancelot. The first time we see them together, Shylock is giving her orders: 'Jessica, my girl,/ Look to my house.' This is because he is going out to dinner with Antonio and Bassanio because he just made a deal with Antonio to lend him money. If he doesn't pay him back in time, Shylock will have a pound of Antonio's flesh.

Reference to plot

Shylock isn't sure whether he wants to spend time with his enemies (though he's pretending to be nice to them) but Jessica wants him to go because she plans to elope with her boyfriend Lorenzo (who is also a Christian) when her father is out. She is a good friend of Lancelot and he is helping her persuade Shylock to go: 'I beseech you, sir, go'. This shows that the relationship between Shylock and Jessica isn't very close.

Valid inference

As it happens, Shylock leaves the house so Jessica, helped by Lancelot, can go ahead with her plot. As Shylock leaves, he gives Jessica strict orders: 'Do as I bid you: shut doors after you.' And she says to herself: 'Farewell – and if my fortune be not crossed, I have a father, you a daughter, lost.' I think this shows how much she hates him.

Personal response – apt inference

Apt reference

Examiner's comments

- This is a lively and engaged start to the Shakespeare part of the task.
- There is awareness of the state of the relationship between Jessica and Shylock.

- There are some apt references to the play's events, supporting the points made.
- To get a higher grade, points need to be developed further. There is a tendency to be dependent on telling the story, rather than discussing the way the characters are speaking and behaving.
- As it stands, this is a Grade C response.

Extract 2 – Grade A response

Strong opening, introducing overview

'Our house is hell,' Jessica says to Lancelot, her father's servant, the first time the audience meets her, and this gives us an immediate impression of her life, and, consequently, her relationship with her father. It is rather poignant that her unhappiness is such that, although she is aware that it is a 'heinous sin ... to be ashamed to be [her] father's child', she is prepared to 'end this strife' by eloping with Lorenzo, a Christian, friend of Bassanio, and therefore, one of her father's sworn enemies.

Sensitive evaluation

Well-noted reference

Yet when we see the way Jessica is treated by her father, it is more than possible to sympathise with her. The only time we see the two characters together is when he is debating whether to go to dinner with Bassanio and Antonio, and is, somewhat reluctantly, leaving her in charge, 'Jessica, my girl,/Look to my house.' Perhaps the fact that he calls her 'my girl' and leaves her in charge of the keys to the house suggests that he trusts her, however he then goes on to give her a long list of how she must behave:

Closely read – probing alternatives

Reference to style

'Clamber not you up to the casements then,/Nor thrust your head into the public street / To gaze on Christian fools with varnished faces; / But stop my house's ears ... Let not the sound of shallow foppery enter / My sober house', and this shows what a cheerless existence she must have.

Supported evaluation

Examiner's comments

- This answer really hits the ground running, with supported evaluation right from the start.
- There is evidence of close and analytical interpretation of detail.
- Assured command of material is evident throughout.
- A cogent and coherent response.
- This is a Grade A response.

HOW TO SUCCEED IN OCR ENGLISH LITERATURE

The Shakespeare task in OCR English Literature will be tested by controlled assessment. This means that you will be required to write your essay on Shakespeare, in school, under controlled conditions using notes you have made earlier.

Examiner's tip
You will be assessed on AO1 in your response to this Shakespeare task. Refer back to page 202 for more details about this assessment objective.

THE TASK AND YOUR RESPONSE

- The task will ask you to show an understanding of Shakespeare's play by referring to particular scenes as they were acted and directed in either a film, staged or audio version of the play that you have watched or heard.

- Your teacher will know what the task is before you start to study the play and will give you advice on how much time you should spend preparing for it. (This time will include formal teaching, research, watching videos/ live performance of the play, writing notes, etc.)

- In total, the final writing of the task is expected to take up to three hours and can be done over more than one session.

- Your final written response should be about 1,000 words.

- You will be allowed to have a clean copy, without annotations, of the play with you while writing your assessment. You can also refer to notes made in advance but these should be short bulleted points, not a full draft essay.

HOW TO GET A GOOD GRADE

- Focus clearly on the terms of the question and ensure that any notes you have made also do this.

- Base your answer on the scene identified in the question but remember to show an understanding of its significance in the play as a whole.

- Show a thorough knowledge of the both the written text and the performed version by using quotations and close reference to details of the performance in your response, wherever relevant. Often short quotations are as effective as long ones, particularly if you embed them fluently into your writing.

Examiner's tip
This Shakespeare task is worth 10 per cent of your total GCSE English Literature exam, so it is worth working hard to get a good grade.

ACTIVITIES

The following activities may help you prepare for writing your response. If possible, work in pairs or small groups so that you can discuss your ideas in full. Remember, you will know the task in advance so make bullet-point notes for reference for when you write your final essay.

Activity 1

The Merchant of Venice is sometimes referred to as one of Shakespeare's 'problem' plays; this is because critics disagree over which characters most deserve our sympathies. In your groups make a list of points for and against having sympathy for the following characters: Shylock, Antonio, Bassanio, Portia, Jessica, and Gratiano.

Activity 2

Think about how the film of the play reflects or alters the view you formed of these characters from reading the text. Do they behave in the way you expected them to? Do the actors speak the words with the same emphasis and intonation that you expect them to? Do their performances reinforce or alter the sympathies that you have for the characters, and why/why not?

Activity 3

Do some research into the attitudes of Shakespeare and his contemporaries towards both Jews and Venice. How far and in what way do their attitudes differ from those of a twenty-first century audience?

> **Examiner's tip**
> Remember, there is no 'right' or 'wrong' way for a Shakespeare play to be performed and produced. However, you must be prepared to justify your own opinions with close reference to the text and to the detail of the film/ stage/audio version.

SAMPLE CONTROLLED ASSESSMENT TASK

> • Remind yourself of Act 4 Scene 1 in the text and in a performed version of the play.
> • Using this scene as a starting point, explore how the characters of Shylock and Portia are portrayed in the performed version you have studied.

Here are extracts from essays by two students who had each watched the Michael Radford film *The Merchant of Venice*.

Extract 1 – Grade C response

<table>
<tr>
<td>Straightforward understanding of Shylock and Antonio's behaviour</td>
<td>At the start of this scene, Shylock is confident that he will take his revenge on Antonio. Al Pacino doesn't rant and rave but seems quite reasonable. Antonio is very quiet and seems to be resigned to his fate. The film shows that the spectators at the trial do not support Shylock, and Gratiano's comments ('O, be thou damned, inexecrable dog!') show their hatred for him.</td>
<td>Clear understan of Gratia role and apt quota</td>
</tr>
<tr>
<td></td>
<td>When the 6,000 ducats are offered to Shylock, there is a brief moment when it seems he might want to take the money; this shows how much gold means to him, but his hatred for Antonio gets the better of him.</td>
<td>A percep comment but does performa show this</td>
</tr>
<tr>
<td>Some awareness of the presentation of character but it needs more</td>
<td>Lynn Collins, who plays Portia, has a false beard and looks quite convincing as a youth. She says the speech ('The quality of mercy is not strained...') in a very reasonable way which makes it sound very convincing but Shylock isn't influenced by it. Overall, the way Shylock is portrayed in this scene helped me understand how his hatred for the Christians influences his behaviour. It also helped me to see how Portia's disguise as a man could be convincing.</td>
<td></td>
</tr>
</table>

Examiner's comments

• This response shows the candidate has a secure knowledge of the text of the play and what happens in it.

• There is a sensible use of appropriate quotations to support the account of the action and a sound awareness of how features of the performed version help to bring out the character's feelings.

• In order to reach a higher grade, the candidate would need to make more specific references to the way Shylock has been portrayed at other points in the play and to the way that the other characters react to him. A more developed explanation of the role of Portia in this scene would also help to raise the grade.

• As it stands, this is a Grade C response.

Extract 2 – Grade A response

At the start of the scene, the Duke orders 'the Jew' to be brought to court. He is not referred to by name and this makes us aware of how the Jews were looked upon by the Venetian society. When he first appears, Shylock can be seen as quite a sympathetic character; in Al Pacino's performance he seems quite calm and reasonable in his request – by his standards he is correct and justified in wanting to keep to the word of his 'bond' and he turns Bassanio's arguments for mercy back on the Christians in his reference to the way the Venetian gentry control the lives of 'many a purchased slave'. At this point, the film shows a pampered Venetian spectator being fanned by his slave and makes us question whether the Venetian–Christian way of life is inherently superior to the values Shylock lives by.

> Awareness of historical/cultural background

> Perceptive awareness of how production reinforces textual implications

> Good use of appropriate quotation

The true Christian values are conveyed through Balthazar's (the disguised Portia's) plea for mercy. Her speech on the quality of mercy is quietly reasonable and spoken thoughtfully, but by now Shylock's blind hatred has been made apparent and her words have no influence on him – any more than they do on Gratiano who continues to show the venomous bigotry towards Shylock that has characterised his behaviour throughout the play ('O, be thou damned, inexecrable dog!').

> [Goo]d, perceptive [und]erstanding [of G]ratiano's [fun]ction in the [play] as a whole

Examiner's comments

- This is a very good critical appreciation of well-selected details of the play and performed version.
- The candidate shows an excellent awareness of how the events of this scene relate to the wider issues of the play as a whole and, in particular, to the complexities of the audience's response to Shylock, and to how far they can sympathise with the attitudes of a character such as Gratiano.
- There is a clear understanding of the text and perceptive explanation of how Shakespeare's language and imagery help to suggest some underlying themes of the play, and how elements of the direction of the film version reinforce the effects of the language.
- This is a Grade A response.